Juvenile Justice and Juvenile Delinquency

Case Studies Workbook

Juvenile Justice and Juvenile Delinquency

Case Studies Workbook

James Windell
Nicole Bain

CRC Press
Taylor & Francis Group
Boca Raton London New York

CRC Press is an imprint of the
Taylor & Francis Group, an **informa** business

CRC Press
Taylor & Francis Group
6000 Broken Sound Parkway NW, Suite 300
Boca Raton, FL 33487-2742

© 2016 by Taylor & Francis Group, LLC
CRC Press is an imprint of Taylor & Francis Group, an Informa business

No claim to original U.S. Government works

Printed on acid-free paper
Version Date: 20150810

International Standard Book Number-13: 978-1-4987-4035-7 (Paperback)

Visit the Taylor & Francis Web site at
http://www.taylorandfrancis.com

and the CRC Press Web site at
http://www.crcpress.com

To my wife, Jane, my daughter, Jill, and my son, Jason.

James Windell

To my husband, Aaron, and my son, Maxwell.

Nicole Bain

And to the thousands of children and teens we got to know in the juvenile justice system over the years. We've always admired their resilience, their ability to overcome adversity, and their emotional resources—that often led to reformation and change.

James Windell and Nicole Bain

Contents

Section I: Juvenile courts and the juvenile justice system

Section II: Juvenile court hearings

Section V: You make the call in other kinds of juvenile court hearings

Section VI: Appeals and the last word

Foreword

James Windell and Nicole Bain's new book provides students and practitioners alike with a step-by-step analysis of the juvenile justice system. As a judge hearing these types of cases every day, I can't emphasize enough the importance of families, clinicians, lawyers, and others involved in juvenile court proceedings to better understand the process. That's why this book is so important. Tapping into their extensive practical juvenile court experience, the authors provide an insightful and fascinating account of the history and evolution of society's attitude toward children and their relationship with the judicial system. A must-read for those who are looking for a practical tool to navigate the complexities and intricacies of the juvenile justice maze, this book delivers as a teaching tool.

The Honorable Lisa Langton
Circuit Court Judge
Sixth Judicial Circuit of Michigan
Pontiac, Michigan

Acknowledgments

There are many people we want to thank for their assistance in writing this book. Some of those people have been kind enough to help directly by offering suggestions and important changes in some of our essential chapters. These recommended changes have made the book more accurate and informative.

Those people who have contributed their expertise and their critical eye include referees Joe Racey, Marty Alvin, Scott Hamilton, and Judge Christopher Dingell. Their kindness in reading chapters and offering comments are deeply appreciated.

Other acknowledgments and thanks go out to friends and colleagues who provided assistance indirectly. They may not know they had a hand in creating and shaping this book, but we would be remiss if we didn't express our gratitude for their contributions. Jim is especially grateful for the 10 years he sat in with court caseworkers and probation officers in their weekly meetings under the supervision of Bill Hamilton. It was instructive to listen—and occasionally offer some input—as they discussed their cases and made collective decisions about how these troubled and delinquent youths should best be handled. Nicole is thankful for her team of fellow caseworkers and supervisors. Regardless of circumstance, they continue to believe in our community's youth and share the desire to help empower them. Often, it's only through a collective effort that the best plans are created and put into action. Their energy, insight, and support have been invaluable.

Since we spent many years in various positions in the Oakland County (Michigan) Family Division and Juvenile Court, we are both grateful to so many people for their kindness, friendship, and the collegial relationships we've enjoyed. These individuals who have been so instrumental in our professional lives include judges, referees, probation officers, psychologists, social workers, and support staff. What we know—and continue to learn—about juvenile courts has come through our contacts and relationships with so many fine people.

Finally, we thank our families for support and encouragement throughout this project.

Authors

James Windell, MA, has been a juvenile court psychologist, an author, a newspaper columnist, an editor, and a criminal justice college instructor. He worked in the juvenile justice system for more than 35 years. Most recently, he was a psychologist in the Oakland County Circuit Court's Family Division, Oakland County, Michigan, doing group therapy with delinquents. He developed a group training program for parents of delinquents that won a national award. Since 2000, he has been an adjunct instructor in the Criminal Justice Department at Wayne State University in Detroit. Since September 2013, he has been a lecturer in criminal justice at Oakland University in Rochester, Michigan. At both universities, he teaches juvenile justice classes.

As a newspaper columnist, Windell wrote the weekly column "Coping With Kids" for the *Oakland Press* and the *Staten Island Advance* for more than 30 years. He published his first book, *Discipline: A Sourcebook of 50 Failsafe Techniques for Parents* (Macmillan) in 1991. Since then, he has written more than 24 books on a variety of subjects. His criminal justice books include *The Student's Guide to Writing a Criminal Justice Research Paper* (Kendall Hunt, 2010), *The American Criminal Justice System* (Cognella, 2013), and *Looking Back in Crime* (CRC Press, 2015).

Nicole Bain has worked in juvenile court and circuit court settings for more than 24 years. She is currently a juvenile court probation officer and worked previously as a juvenile diversion coordinator, victim's advocate, and a paralegal for a prosecuting attorney's office. She has managed caseloads of juvenile delinquents, conducted training and informative workshops for teen volunteers regarding the juvenile court and diversion programs, and counseled families and children through court processes and testifying. Bain has had daily, first-hand experience and involvement with juvenile offenders for the past 10 years—often maintaining month-long to several year-long relationships with them, their families, their school, the court, and their specific group of support professionals. She has researched and recommended juvenile rehabilitative programming to the court and supervised adjudicated youth throughout their treatment. She has maintained working relationships among the court bench, as well as with professionals in local mental health agencies and with agents from various statewide juvenile residential programs. She has lectured in college classes regarding the juvenile justice system, delinquency, restorative justice, and the work of probation officers.

Introduction

In the juvenile court, referees, judges, and other court personnel have to constantly make decisions that affect the lives of children and their families. That's not like it is in adult criminal courts, where there are sentencing guidelines and mandatory/minimum sentences that provide judges with guidelines and constraints. If an adult offender is convicted, it is known ahead of time what the sentence is likely to be—or at least, the range that the punishment will fall in.

Not so in juvenile or family courts. Juvenile courts were founded in this country on the principle that children and adolescents are fundamentally different than adults and that in order to protect and save them from a life of crime, they must be treated as individuals. Each child is different and the background and unique characteristics of each minor must be taken into consideration in order that the disposition (the equivalent of sentencing in the adult criminal system) is tailored to the particular child and his or her best interests. In the adult system, the concern is protecting society; in the juvenile system, the greater concern is protecting the child.

Although in the more than 100 years since the establishment of juvenile courts in the United States more formality has been introduced in juvenile courts, still the juvenile court is a place in which juvenile offenders and their families are accorded special services. There are no mandatory sentences. There are no proscribed absolutes for juvenile court dispositions. Juvenile court judges and referees can be as creative as they choose to be; the goal always is to rehabilitate and treat a child so that he or she will grow up to a law-abiding citizen. How referees and judges, as well as other court staff, go about doing that is the subject of this book.

This book is designed to give you—whether you want to learn more about juvenile and family courts and their dispositions or you are a student in a criminal justice class—an opportunity to experience, in a more hands-on manner, what it is like to face decisions in the juvenile court system. Written in a workbook style, this book will give you the chance to see information about actual cases and make decisions about young people and their futures.

You will be given case scenarios that range from cases at the juvenile court intake level all the way to those related to making decisions as to whether a young person should be waived into the criminal system to be tried as an adult felon. You can discuss and argue the circumstances and situations of children and their families, and you can try to be as creative as possible to try to save each young person from more delinquency and crime. Then, after you have made your decision, you will be able to compare your dispositional choices with those of the actual judge or referee. But you will also get information as to the outcome. What happened to this young person in the year or so after the court handed down a disposition? Was he or she successful in staying out of more trouble? Or was the disposition handed down by the real judge and referee inadequate in helping the young person to change his or her life? Would your recommendations have made a difference?

Finally, in each chapter of this book, you will learn more about the juvenile justice system. You will be given statistics, facts, court decisions, and information about policies that will enable you to have a better understanding of the juvenile justice system. While you are deciding on dispositions for the juveniles described in this book, you will learn more about the laws, policies, and historical events that have shaped the juvenile court into the system we have today.

section one

Juvenile courts and the juvenile justice system

chapter one

Invention of the juvenile court

When the juvenile court was invented and implemented in Chicago at the end of the nineteenth century, its main role was to intervene in the lives of children. But the road to achieving a public agency to deal with the problems of children was a long and arduous one.

Up until the nineteenth century—and the end of that century at that—children had not been viewed as needing their own court, and the court that finally took shape on the eve of the twentieth century resembled an extension of the social welfare system, rather than the court system that already existed for adults.

How did we get to that point and why was it finally decided that a separate court for children and youth was necessary? And why was a court for minors developed in the United States?

These questions can only be addressed if we consider the history of our civilization and the evolution over thousands of years of mankind's attitudes toward children. Certainly, in the late 1800s, it involved the bringing together of separate strains.

Paul Lerman, a former professor of social work and sociology at Rutgers University and the author of books and articles on youth, sees the three strains that came together, leading to the establishment of juvenile courts, as the adult correctional system, juvenile corrections (including reform schools and training schools), and the child welfare development of shelters, cottages, and facilities for neglected and dependent youth. These three different developments took shape mostly in the nineteenth century, but, before that, there was rarely any emphasis on the special needs of young people.

Throughout history, both adults and children who violated the norms and laws of society were generally dealt with in the same manner. That is, they went to the same courts, and were punished in the same ways—which often meant whipping, mutilation, banishment, torture, and execution.

That's not to say that children were never thought of as different from adults. They were, at times. For instance, in the fifth century, the age for determining whether minors would be exempted from criminal responsibility was set at age seven. Indeed, throughout recorded history, at least until about the eighteenth century, children at age seven or sometimes younger were expected to accept adult roles. Children in poor families were frequently apprenticed in crafts and trades to wealthy families. Landowners, especially in England,

assumed control over children and their welfare, and the traditions that grew out of these practices influenced the shaping of the juvenile justice system in Great Britain.

Chancery courts

Early in English history, both Chancery courts and the concept of *parens patriae* evolved. Both played a vital role in the juvenile justice system that would ultimately emerge, not only in England but also in the United States as well.

Chancery courts in the twelfth and thirteenth centuries were responsible for performing many tasks. They managed children and their affairs, and they were the courts that would deal with the mentally ill and the incompetent. Essentially, Chancery courts were courts that in early English Common Law were where conflicts and disputes related to children could be resolved.

Parens patriae

Parens patriae, which literally translates as "parent of the country," is a concept that originated with the King of England, during the twelfth century. This idea of the father of the country, when applied to juvenile matters, means that the king was responsible for all the children. That is, the king could make decisions about—and for—all children in the kingdom.

English Common Law viewed parents as being responsible for the upbringing of their children. However, as children grew older—particularly beyond age seven—parents were less actively involved in their child's life, and the child had to be accountable to the state. Chancellors, acting for the king, adjudicated matters involving juveniles and the offenses they committed. Children had no legal rights or standing in any court. To a large degree, children were wards of the court, and it was the court that was responsible for their well-being.

Because children were under the protective control of the king, it was not difficult for English kings to justify intervention in their lives. The doctrine of *parens patriae* could justify any intervention.

While children under age seven were not held responsible for their crimes, those older than seven were. There were as many as 200 crimes for which children in England could be executed. In the late eighteenth century, it was common for kids between 8 and 14 to be hanged or transported to another country as punishment for one of these capital offenses.

Juvenile justice in the United States

It may be expected, since many early settlers in the United States came from England, that many juveniles were handled, during the early colonial days in the New World, just as they would have been in England. For the most part, parents were responsible for their children's behavior. When a child violated the law, usually the parents administered punishment. However, there were exceptions. The violations of some laws—such as those pertaining to running away from their masters or from their parents, being incorrigible, lying, swearing, fighting, stealing, or cheating—could be punished by the community. That would often mean that they would be whipped much like they would have been at home.

As in England, children were put to work at an early age, and then they became part of the labor force. Often they were indentured or apprenticed out to work for someone else, which helped to lessen the burden on the family. In the labor force, they were watched closely, and there was less time and opportunity for them to get into serious trouble.

But still, children after the age of seven could be punished or even put to death. Very few children were actually executed, although it happened on occasion, and, indeed, the threat was constantly there. The more frequent punishments for children and adolescents were public whippings and placement in debtor's prisons. The conditions in these prisons, which held a conglomeration of adult criminals, the mentally ill, and incompetents, were very poor and quite inhumane.

An age of reform

As the New World moved into the nineteenth century, there were concerns about the correctional system—such as it was—both for adults and children. Reformers began to call for changes in the way criminal offenders were handled. After the United States became independent, the country was free to go its own way without emulating England. The new country wanted to be different from England, and one way to show this independence was in terms of how it would deal with law violators. In Pennsylvania, for instance, there was opposition to the old ways of doing things. Public punishments and hangings were decried, with critics of the old way calling for private punishment and increased use of jails. Jails should be different, the reformers said, and they should be much more humane. This kind of advocacy resulted in the penitentiary system and the first American prisons.

In the area of juvenile justice, the reforms were led by religious groups that showed concerns about juvenile delinquents as well as the poor and homeless—or at least unsupervised—children. The English Common Law doctrine of *parens patriae* was interpreted in a strictly American style, when, in 1820, the Society for the Reformation of Juvenile Delinquents was formed. The goal of this organization was to bring to the public's attention the vast number of "unfortunate children" from 10 to 18 years of age who roamed the streets breaking laws. Society saw these children as lacking good parenting and, thus, they were—the society observed—frequently making hasty and ill-considered decisions; which, of course, upset the society, which wanted the state to intervene to help these wayward children. The state should take over the parenting of children when the parents were not doing a good enough job. If parents weren't properly raising their children, then the state should step in and take over. This was the American way of extending the idea of *parens patriae*: Get involved in the lives of children when their parents were not raising them properly. In effect, they were urging the government to take control over how parents raise their children.

As a result of the clamoring for action by the Society for the Reformation of Juvenile Delinquents and other groups, facilities and institutions were established to house boys and girls in their own best interest. One of the earliest of these institutions was the House of Refuge, which opened in New York in 1825. The House of Refuge took in both delinquent youth, who previously would have been incarcerated with adults, as well as neglected and abandoned children, who were in danger of becoming juvenile delinquents. While the House of Refuge separated children from adults, it wasn't much of a refuge or sanctuary for kids. Discipline was harsh, children could be placed in solitary confinement, and food could be withheld from them.

Although some parents challenged the groups or the government taking control of their children, the courts supported the concept of *parens patriae* and said that children were being held—and, indeed, confined—to reform them, not to punish them.

The child savers

When institutions such as the House of Refuge tended to morph into institutions that became overcrowded and abusive, they were, at the same time, evolving into somewhat more punitive reform schools. Reform schools were, for the most part, prisons for juveniles. Children were, in fact, removed from abusive home conditions, "saved" from lives of delinquency, and separated from adult criminals. Yet, these children, placed in reform schools, were still imprisoned.

By the midpoint of the nineteenth century, the Massachusetts State Industrial School for Girls was opened as the first girls' reformatory. This development reflected a growing concern about delinquent and abused girls, but, again, it was another move toward imprisonment of children—only this time it was the imprisonment of girls.

But by the 1870s and 1880s, there was a new wave of social interest in America's young criminals as the "child savers" movement began.

The child savers were mostly women from the white middle class, who were well-educated, politically active, and engaged in community service and other worthy causes (Oliver and Hilgenberg, 2006). They were trying to provide lodging, food, and clothing for the children on the streets, but there were far too many to effectively help. One solution that was utilized for a number of years was placing children on "orphan trains" and shipping them out west, where they would presumably be exposed to a more pleasant and healthy environment as compared to the one they were removed from in industrialized cities. Not everyone saw what the child savers were trying to do as benevolent or benign. Critics of the child savers contend that much of the work of the child savers was an attempt to impose middle-class, Protestant values on a group of Catholic immigrant children of lower socioeconomic status (Mays and Winfree, 2000).

Whatever the motivations of the child savers might have been, during the last decade of the nineteenth century, groups representing the law, philanthropic societies, and the newly emerging profession of social work, all came together to advocate for something new for delinquent children: their own special court (Mays and Winfree, 2000).

By 1895, groups like the Chicago Women's Club were formulating ideas. Why not a court for juveniles, they asked. And the Chicago Women's Club followed this up by drafting a bill and sending it to the Illinois legislature. However, it was not passed. But, it seemed to ignite political interest in a juvenile court, and subsequently, four years later, the Illinois legislature passed the Illinois Juvenile Court Act of 1899. This law created a juvenile court, a court that had jurisdiction over children charged with crimes.

In addition, the new juvenile court was given jurisdiction over

> Any child who for any reason is destitute or homeless or abandoned; or dependent on the public for support; or has no proper parental care or guardianship; or who habitually begs or receives alms; or who is living in any house of ill fame or with any vicious or disreputable person; or whose home by reason of neglect,

cruelty, or depravity on the part of its parents, guardian or any other person in whose care it may be, is an unfit place for such a child; and any child under the age of 8 who is found peddling or selling any article or singing or playing a musical instrument upon the street or giving any public entertainment (Oliver and Hilgenberg, 2006, p. 205).

The Illinois Juvenile Court Act of 1899 was unique in that it not only created a separate court for children and youth, but it defined a rehabilitative purpose for a court—rather than the traditional punishment purposes. Furthermore, the Act established that juvenile court records would be confidential so as to minimize stigma, and it required that juveniles be separated from adults when placed in the same institution. Finally, it was a unique law that provided for the informality of juvenile court procedures.

By 1912, 22 states had passed legislation similar to the Illinois Juvenile Court Act of 1899. And, by 1925, that number would increase to 46 states and the District of Columbia. So, within 26 years, the juvenile court system had become a fixed and wholly separate part of the court system in the United States. It would remain that way until the 1960s.

LEARNING MORE

After 1899, the new juvenile court system blossomed. However, this new system was not without its problems. For instance, in 1905, the case of *Commonwealth v. Fischer* (213 Pa. 48) was brought before the Pennsylvania Supreme Court specifically to discuss one question: What due process protections were allowed juveniles?

The case revolved around 14-year-old Frank Fischer, who was placed in the Philadelphia House of Refuge after being convicted of larceny. After he was sentenced, his father objected to his son's sentence, pointing out that his son received a sentence more severe than if he had been convicted and sentenced in an adult criminal court.

The Philadelphia Supreme Court upheld the juvenile court's decision, noting that the state may place a child in a house of refuge if the family is unwilling to control the juvenile's actions and that due process protections were unnecessary when the state operates under its *parens patriae* powers. In supporting the juvenile court's purpose, the Pennsylvania Supreme Court illustrated how the court's role in training delinquent children superseded the rights of children and their parents:

> The design is not punishment, nor the restraint imprisonment, any more than is the wholesome restraint which a parent exercises over his child.... Every statute which is designed to give protection, care, and training to children, as a parental duty, is but a recognition of the duty of the state, as the legitimate guardian and protector of children where other guardianship fails. No constitutional right is violated (*Commonwealth v. Fisher*, 213, Pa. 48, 1905).

FOR FURTHER CONSIDERATION

Questions for discussion

1. Why was the age of seven selected as the minimum age of reason centuries ago? Does this jibe with the latest brain research?
2. Have juvenile courts lost their purpose over the years? Why or why not?

Review for chapter one

Important terms to know:

Criminal responsibility: Having criminal liability for one's actions. Children under age seven in English Common Law were excluded from criminal liability as it was believed they were incapable of forming intent for criminal actions.

Chancery Courts: Chancery Courts in the twelfth and thirteenth centuries were responsible for managing children and their affairs, and they were the one court that would deal with the mentally ill and the incompetent.

Parens patriae: A Latin term meaning parent of the country; applied to juvenile matters, the term means that the king was responsible for all of the

children. In more contemporary times, it means that the state is responsible for and can make decisions for children in certain circumstances.

English Common Law: The body of customary law, based upon judicial decisions and embodied in reports of case decisions, that had been administered by the common-law courts of England beginning in the Middle Ages.

Child savers: The child savers were mostly women in nineteenth century United States from the white middle-class, who were well-educated, politically active, and engaged in community service and other worthy causes, but took a special interest in saving wayward children.

Illinois Juvenile Court Act of 1899: The Act that created the first juvenile court in America.

Study guide questions

Choose the right answers from the choices below.

1. Throughout history, up to the nineteenth century, children who violated the law were treated as
   a. Mentally incompetent
   b. Adults
   c. Minor children
   d. The insane
2. Both Chancery courts and the concept of _____ played a vital role in the juvenile justice system that would ultimately develop in England and America.
   a. The common law
   b. Crime control
   c. *Parens patriae*
   d. Criminal justice
3. During the last part of the nineteenth century, groups representing the law, philanthropic societies, and the newly emerging profession of social work, all came together to advocate for something new for delinquent children:
   a. A juvenile court
   b. Penal institutions for children
   c. A society to prevent cruelty to children
   d. Orphan trains to send delinquents away

chapter two

The juvenile justice process

As you learned in chapter one, juvenile courts were specifically designed to operate under highly informal proceedings that dispensed with the procedural formalities that would be found in other courts.

Judge Julian Mack, one of the early juvenile court judges in Cook County, Illinois, writing in the *Harvard Law Review* in 1909, said this about the court's goals:

> The child who must be brought into court should, of course, be made to know that he is face to face with the power of the state, but he should at the same time, and more emphatically, be made to feel that he is the object of its care and solicitude. The ordinary trappings of the courtroom are out of place in such hearings. The judge on a bench, looking down upon the boy standing at the bar, can never evoke a proper sympathetic spirit. Seated at a desk, with the child at his side, where he can on occasion put his arm around his shoulder and draw the lad to him, the judge, while losing none of his judicial disposition, will gain immensely in the effectiveness of his work (Mack, 1909, p. 120).

Juvenile court proceedings, therefore, were derived from the doctrine of *parens patriae*—the state acting in the role of the benevolent parent—and the goal was treatment, rather than punishment. A primary objective, as can be found in Judge Mack's statement, is to protect children, while creating a safe and nurturing environment for them in the courtroom—and, indeed, throughout the rehabilitative process. Punishment, revenge, and retribution were considered unnecessary and unproductive in juvenile courts. In brief, it was a treatment court—not a criminal court.

In order for the juvenile court to be an informal court pursuing treatment, it had to shed other aspects of criminal courts besides the judge's traditional black robe and the high benches. The terminology used in adult criminal courts also had to be altered.

For example, the new vocabulary of the juvenile court was petition, instead of complaint; adjudication instead of conviction; disposition instead of sentencing; and commitment, instead of imprisonment.

But there were other important differences between the criminal court and the juvenile court. In most states, there was no bail for juveniles who were detained. And the children's identity would be safeguarded—rather than being released to the public via the media. Also, referees could hear cases, instead of judges.

Perhaps one of the most essential differences between the juvenile court and the adult system—even today—is the way responsibility is viewed. Most juvenile offenders are considered victims of circumstances out of their control—not as guilty perpetrators who have acted based on their own free will (del Carmen and Trulson, 2006). Usually, adult offenders are seen as rational individuals who deserve blame for their criminal acts. Children, on the other hand, are seen as being victims of their home lives and their own mental and emotional immaturity.

The process of the juvenile justice system reflects the difference in the way juvenile offenders are viewed. And that starts when they are arrested by a police officer. In fact, juveniles who have been arrested are not said to be arrested. Rather, they are "taken into custody." The police (as well as any other adult) can file a petition alleging a criminal violation; but it is a petition—not a criminal complaint. And when the prosecutor brings charges against a juvenile, they file a petition with the juvenile court. It is not an indictment or an information (a formal, written, criminal accusation drawn up by a prosecutor setting out the charges for which the defendant must stand trial; an information replaces the indictment in many states).

Most juvenile court proceedings follow the same procedures:

- *Preadjudication*: An adult files a petition with the juvenile court intake department. The intake department, or the intake hearing officer, decides to take the case, handle it informally, refer it to another social agency, or to drop it altogether.
- *Adjudication*: This phase is similar to the trial period in a criminal court. A hearing is held in which evidence is presented before the juvenile court and the judge or referee decides whether a delinquent act has occurred. Hearsay evidence is acceptable, and the juvenile is allowed to address the court on his or her own behalf. After hearing the evidence, it is the responsibility of the judge or referee to review that evidence and accept or reject the allegations in the petition.

- *Disposition*: A disposition is a hearing held after the adjudication. This is similar to sentencing in the adult criminal system. The judge or referee decides what sanctions the juvenile is to receive. The disposition can involve detention or commitment, removal from the parent's home, restitution, treatment, or probation.
- *Postdisposition*: If the juvenile is placed on probation, he or she is assigned to a probation officer. However, even if the youth is placed in a residential facility or a different home, the probation officer will still play an essential role in providing aftercare, supervision, and assistance with pursuing a satisfactory adjustment in the community.

Having reviewed the basic procedures of the juvenile court, in the next chapter we will look at who the juvenile court has jurisdiction over.

FOR FURTHER CONSIDERATION
Questions for discussion
1. Do juvenile courts still provide what Judge Julian Mack suggested is essential for juvenile courts?
2. Does our society continue to believe that juvenile offenders are victims of society?

Review for chapter two
Important terms to know:

Taken into custody: Instead of juveniles being arrested, the juvenile justice system prefers to say that children are taken into custody.

Adjudication: The term for a trial in juvenile courts.
Disposition: The term that replaces sentencing in juvenile courts.

Study guide questions
Choose the right answers from the choices below.

1. Judge Julian Mack, writing in the *Harvard Law Review* in 1909, said this about the juvenile court's goals:
   a. The child should know who is boss.
   b. The child should be made to feel afraid.
   c. The child should be made to feel that he is the object of the juvenile court's care and solicitude.
   d. The child should be in awe of the authority of the juvenile court's power.
2. Perhaps one of the most essential differences between the juvenile court and the adult system—even today—is the way
   a. Responsibility is viewed.
   b. Juvenile offenders are seen as little monsters.
   c. Juvenile offenders are viewed as having made their own decisions.
   d. Juvenile offenders are seen as guilty perpetrators who have acted based on their own free will.
3. This phase is similar to the trial period in a criminal court:
   a. Pretrial
   b. Intake hearing
   c. Disposition
   d. Adjudication

section two

Juvenile court hearings

chapter three

Scope of the juvenile justice system

Who does the juvenile court have jurisdiction over?

First and foremost, the juvenile court can take jurisdiction over juveniles. Second, it has jurisdiction over juvenile offenders. And third, it can impose sanctions on parents of juveniles who are offenders as well as over those parents who have been found to be neglectful, abusive, or who have failed to properly care for their children in many other ways.

Who is a juvenile?

Just as each state has passed a state law authorizing a juvenile court and defining the term *delinquency*, each state has also set the age for who gets defined as a juvenile. There is, in every state, a minimum and a maximum age determined by legislation. If the individual is above the maximum age, he or she is considered an adult and is processed in the adult criminal justice system.

When comparing the maximum ages around the 50 states, the most common maximum age is 17. This means that if a youth commits a criminal act when he or she is 17 or younger, he or she will be subjected to the jurisdiction of the juvenile court. If he or she is 18 or older when the offense occurs, he or she will be tried in an adult court.

In three states (Connecticut, New York, and North Carolina), the maximum age is 15, which means that 16-year-olds who violate the law are subjected to the jurisdiction of adult courts. There are other states that have set the maximum age at 16.

Although every state has a maximum age for defining a juvenile, not every state has a minimum age. You will recall that in English Common Law children under the age of seven were presumed to be unable to develop intent and, therefore, they could not be prosecuted for their behavior.

Sixteen states have set a minimum age for jurisdiction in the juvenile court. All of those states have established that minimum age at between 6 and 10. For example, Arizona has decreed that the minimum age should be eight. Consequently, any child aged seven or younger who commits a delinquent act cannot be brought into a juvenile court. In effect, this means that in Arizona a 7-year-old who commits a murder could only be released into the custody of his or her parents.

On the other hand, there are states, such as California and Michigan, which have no minimum age

for the juvenile court to assume jurisdiction. By law, in these states, a youngster as young as four or five could be brought before a juvenile court for a delinquency hearing.

Who is a juvenile delinquent?

While this seems like a fairly simple question, it is actually somewhat more complex than it seems.

Generally, in our society, we define juvenile delinquency in two separate ways—there's a social definition and a legal definition.

Often, we view young people as juvenile delinquents when they are disorderly, unruly, and cause trouble. In other words, many people casually toss out the term *juvenile delinquent* to refer to any child or adolescent who fail to follow rules, is disrespectful to authority, and seems to have little regard for social conventions.

But there is also a legal definition which is more precise and, for the purposes of this book, should be used. That is, legally, a juvenile delinquent is any minor who has come under the jurisdiction of a juvenile court. Technically, a youth becomes a juvenile delinquent when he or she has gone through the adjudication process in the juvenile court and been found guilty of a delinquent offense. Just being accused of a delinquent act or having a petition filed against him or her does not make a juvenile a delinquent.

Juvenile offenders

Each state also defines what is delinquency in that state. In general, delinquency is usually defined in a state's statutes as any violation of local, state, or federal criminal laws. However, delinquency usually consists of two categories: (1) any act that, if committed by an adult, would be a crime and (2) any act that would not be a violation of the criminal code if committed by an adult, but nonetheless falls under the definition of delinquency for minors. Acts in this second category are called status offenses.

States do not list criminal offenses by the age of the actor. Robbery, burglary, or murder, for example, are crimes no matter the age of the offender (at least if the offender is over the minimum age as determined in that state). An adult committing one of these crimes will go before a criminal court; a juvenile committing one of these offenses will go before a juvenile court. Delinquent acts have to be committed by individuals who fall within the age designated by the state and include crimes against persons, crimes against property, drug offenses, and crimes against the public order (Office of Juvenile Justice and Delinquency Prevention, 1998).

But there is that second category of offenses known as status offenses. These are actions that would not be considered a crime if committed by an adult. Common status offenses include skipping school, running away from home, smoking a tobacco product, and being incorrigible (not obeying the rules and being out of the control of parents).

About half of all states classify status offenders as delinquents. The other states classify status offenders as children in need of supervision (CHINS) or Minors in Need of Supervision (MINS), or some similar designation.

In some states, therefore, a minor who runs away from home or is caught drinking alcohol might go before the juvenile court with the possibility of being adjudicated as a delinquent.

Status offenses have been of concern both in local jurisdictions as well as at the national level, mainly because there is concern about the potential stigma that goes along with being declared a delinquent. This is especially true, it is argued, if the child is adjudicated a delinquent without having broken a criminal law (at least a law that applied to adults). The Office of Juvenile Justice and Delinquency Prevention (OJJDP), an office within the Department of Justice, has been working for many years to try to make sure that status offenders who come into the juvenile justice system are not exposed to delinquents or are not placed in detention with delinquents.

Adolescents who engage in status offense behaviors often come from broken homes, have suffered childhood trauma, and have unmet mental health and/or education needs (Arthur and Waugh, 2009). Experts contend that these troubled children need care, treatment, and services—not confinement—to address the underlying causes of their troubling behavior and to prevent deeper and more costly entanglement in the juvenile or criminal justice systems. In 1974, Congress passed the Juvenile Justice and Delinquency Prevention Act prohibiting the placement of status offenders in secure confinement. Unfortunately, this prohibition has been significantly undermined by a 1980 amendment to the Act that allows the detention of status offenders for violations of a valid court order. A valid court order might be an order, entered by a judge in a dependency or status offense proceeding, commanding a juvenile to desist from specified noncriminal behavior. For example, a foster youth may be ordered at a dependency review hearing to stop running away from a placement, or a truant may be ordered to stop running away from home.

As a result, thousands of status offenders are in secure residential facilities on any given day in the United States (Arthur and Waugh, 2009).

Jurisdiction over parents

Juvenile courts also have jurisdiction over dependent and neglected children. Neglected, abused, and dependent children come to the attention of the juvenile justice system because parents or guardians have failed to provide for them in safe or healthy ways.

Dependency results when parents or guardians are absent, often through death, imprisonment, or disability. Neglect occurs when a parent or guardian fails to provide physical, emotional, or financial support, and in some cases, neglect includes abandonment or abuse.

The juvenile court has jurisdiction over children who are neglected, abused, or dependent. But the court also has a measure of jurisdiction over parents in dependency, neglect, abuse, and delinquency cases as well. Juvenile courts can sanction parents who have contributed to the delinquency of their child, and they can impose requirements or penalties on parents, which could range from fines to jail time. For example, parents of delinquents can be ordered to take parenting classes, attend Alcoholics Anonymous groups, or go for family counseling. When children are placed by the court in a residential facility, parents can be ordered by the court to pay for the placement. In some situations, the juvenile court can remove the children from the care of the parents or even permanently terminate the rights of parents.

In some states, the juvenile court is located within the family court; it is alternatively called the family court, domestic relations court, or the probate court. These alternative names reflect the broad jurisdiction these courts have over many matters involving juveniles.

Family courts actually began just after the development of the juvenile court, as reformers turned their attention to families. Starting in Cincinnati, Ohio, in 1914, courts with jurisdiction over both children and families began to be established in various cities around the United States (Jackson and Knepper, 2003). But it wasn't until 1959 that three working groups collaborated to produce the Standard Family Court Act to assist states interested in family courts (Jackson and Knepper, 2003). After this Act was published, several states created family courts. Rhode Island began its family court in 1961, New York in 1962, and Hawaii in 1965. Since the 1960s, several other states have adopted family court systems.

The central idea of the family court is that, rather than shuffle family matters from court to court to resolve disputes, all matters related to a single family would be heard by a family court judge according to the "one judge, one family" principle (Jackson and Knepper, 2003). While family courts differ, their jurisdiction may include marital actions, juvenile proceedings, adoptions, paternity suits, civil commitments, protection orders, and criminal cases resulting from domestic violence.

Roscoe Pound, Dean of the Harvard Law School between 1916 and 1936 and an early advocate of family courts, put it this way:

> Treating the family situation as a series of single controversies may often not do justice to the whole or the several parts. The several parts are likely to be distorted in considering them apart from the whole, and the whole may be left undetermined in a series of adjudications of the parts (Pound, 1959, p. 164).
>
> Some advocates of family courts contend that if family problems are left unresolved, they tend to develop into larger problems of delinquency and family violence (Jackson and Knepper, 20903). When family courts use nonadversarial means of dispute resolution in delinquency matters there is a much better chance of resolution without adverse results. Nonadversarial strategies include judicial conferences, neighborhood dispute committees, intake service conferences, and programs utilizing teen courts (youth courts or peer courts where teens administer diversion alternatives to other teen offenders).

IDEAS TO CONSIDER

In this chapter, we discussed who is a juvenile, and what is juvenile delinquency. However, since this book is about the juvenile justice system, it seems important to ask a further question: What is justice?

We have all said many times in the Pledge of Allegiance that we pledge allegiance to the flag of the United States of America, and we conclude by saying, "…with liberty and justice to all." That sounds good, but what exactly is justice? And when we talk about the juvenile *justice* system, what do we mean?

Aristotle wrote several thousand years ago that the *just* is that which is lawful and that which is fair and equal. Today, many people believe that justice is an ideal concerning the maintenance of rights and the correction of wrongs in our society (Champion, 2001). But justice can mean the proper and appropriate administration of the laws (Garner, 2000). Jack Handler in *Ballentine's Law Dictionary* (1994) defines justice as "the goal of a society which demands that its courts diligently apply its laws to the facts of each case, in every case" (p. 287).

> Perhaps we can conclude that the juvenile justice system is an apparatus that our society uses to enforce the standards of conduct necessary to protect children, while concurrently safeguarding the community. The implications of calling it the juvenile *justice* system is that all children and their families are treated fairly no matter who they are, no matter their gender, no matter their race, no matter their religion, and no matter where they live.

FOR FURTHER CONSIDERATION
Questions for discussion
1. What should be the age at which a youth is considered an adult for criminal prosecution purposes? Why?
2. What kind of jurisdiction should juvenile courts have over parents?
3. Under what circumstances should juvenile courts be able to order parents to take certain actions?

Review for chapter three
Important terms to know:

Juvenile delinquent: A juvenile delinquent is any minor who has come under the jurisdiction of a juvenile court. Technically, a youth becomes a juvenile delinquent when he or she has gone through the adjudication process in the juvenile court and been found guilty of a delinquent offense.

Status offense: These are actions which would not be considered a crime if committed by an adult, such as running away or cutting classes at school.

Neglect: Neglect occurs when a parent or guardian fails to provide physical, emotional, or financial support to a child.

Study guide questions
Choose the right answers from the choices below.

1. In each state, legislation determines the minimum and maximum ages for a youth to be considered
   a. A delinquent
   b. An adult
   c. A parent
   d. A grandparent
2. When comparing the maximum ages of a youth to be considered a delinquent among the 50 states, the most common maximum age is
   a. 12
   b. 15

c. 16

d. 17

3. In general, delinquency is usually defined in each state's statutes as

   a. Any violation of local, state, or federal criminal laws

   b. Behavior that is obnoxious

   c. Any actions that trouble parents or teachers

   d. Any violation of basic decency

4. An example of a status offense would be

   a. Failing to go to church on Sunday

   b. Getting failing grades at school

   c. Smoking a tobacco product

   d. Watching too much television

5. The word justice often means

   a. That which is lawful and that which is fair and equal

   b. An ideal concerning the maintenance of rights and the correction of wrongs in our society

   c. The proper and appropriate administration of the laws

   d. All of the above

chapter four

What rights do juveniles have in the juvenile court?

In the 1960s, Americans began to question the validity and the efficiency of the juvenile court. The informality and focus on treatment of the juvenile court was said by some critics to have been given greater importance than the due process rights of juveniles.

There were two conflicting sets of voices in the debate over the juvenile court in the 1960s. One set of voices, often said to be from those who were identified as politically conservative, complained that juvenile courts were too lenient on aggressive and violent delinquents, and that juvenile courts were incapable of dealing with dangerous youth. On the other side were those who were decidedly more liberal, who took the position that the constitutional rights of juveniles were being ignored or—at times—even trampled on by juvenile courts.

Prior to 1966, the U.S. Supreme Court rarely heard any cases raising issues with regards to the power of the juvenile court or the rights of juveniles. But that was to change in 1966, when the Supreme Court decided the case of *Kent v. United States.*

This was a case from Washington, DC, in which 16-year-old Morris Kent was transferred by a juvenile judge from the juvenile court to an adult court without holding a hearing. And, in addition, the judge did not provide Kent's attorney with social information that the judge used to make his decision. After hearing oral arguments, the Supreme Court, with Associate Justice Abe Fortas writing for the majority, concluded that Morris Kent had been denied due process. The high court stated that counsel in a juvenile case must be provided meaningful information and that a juvenile was entitled to a hearing to determine a transfer to an adult criminal court. Furthermore, the decision held that the judge, in ordering such a transfer, must accompany the decision for a transfer with a statement spelling out the reasons for that transfer. In his written opinion, Fortas issued an ominous warning:

> There is evidence, in fact, that there may be grounds for concern that the child receives the worst of both worlds; that he gets neither the protections accorded to adults nor the solicitous care and regenerative treatment postulated for children (*Kent v. United States*, 1966).

The very next year, the U.S. Supreme Court issued another decision which shed more light on Fortas' ominous warning given in the Kent decision. In the case called *In re Gault*, the court issued its most resounding declaration regarding the need for reform in the juvenile courts so that the rights of juveniles would not be neglected.

As a result of this one case and the Supreme Court's decision, which was again written by Associate Justice Abe Fortas, the nature of the juvenile court would be radically changed.

The case seemed simple enough. A 15-year-old Gerald Gault and a buddy, both Arizona teens, were taken into custody by the police for allegedly making obscene phone calls. However, what happened after that would not be so simple; it was, in many respects, a legal and due process nightmare.

Gault's parents were not told that their son was taken into custody and that he was being held in a detention center. Then, there was no formal notice given to the parents of the charges against Gerald and no formal notice of when the court hearing would be held. Furthermore, Gerald and his parents were not informed that he did not have to testify against himself, nor that he had a right to an attorney. When the hearing was held, no witnesses were called to present evidence against Gerald, which meant that Gerald did not have the ability to confront or cross-examine witnesses against him. And, finally, when the judge committed Gerald to an indeterminate number of years in an Industrial School, the family discovered that there was no right to an appeal for juvenile court cases in Arizona.

The U.S. Supreme Court overturned the Arizona court's disposition of Gerald Gault. In the decision, the high court held that children had rights. The Supreme Court stated that Gerald Gault had the following rights:

- The right to an attorney
- The right to confront his accusers and the right to cross-examine them
- The right against self-incrimination
- The right to have timely notice of the charges against him
- The right to appellate review (*In re Gault*, 1967)

The Supreme Court concluded that the original purposes of the juvenile court—that a fatherly judge would look into each situation thoroughly and prescribe a treatment plan to save a juvenile from a life of crime—were not being served (Taylor and Fritsch, 2011).

The Supreme Court acknowledged that due process requirements would introduce more order, formality, and maybe even more elements of an adversarial system; however, the Supreme Court ruled that the juvenile court could still retain some of the best aspects of its kindly and therapeutic nature. In rendering his opinion, Justice Fortas quoted from the *Challenge of Crime in a Free Society*, a report that had recently been issued, following a study of crime in America:

> Fears have been expressed that lawyers would make juvenile court proceedings adversary [adversarial]. No doubt this is partly true, but it is partly desirable. Informality is often abused. The juvenile courts deal with cases in which facts are disputed and in which, therefore, rules of evidence, confrontation of witnesses, and other adversary [adversarial] procedures are called for. They deal with many cases involving conduct that can lead to incarceration or close supervision for long periods, and therefore juveniles often need the same safeguards that are granted to adults. And in all cases children need advocates to speak for them and guard their interests, particularly when disposition decisions are made. It is the disposition stage at which the opportunity arises to offer individualized treatment plans and in which the danger inheres that the court's coercive power will be applied without adequate knowledge of the circumstances.
>
> Fears also have been expressed that the formality lawyers would bring into juvenile court would defeat the therapeutic aims of the court. But informality has no necessary connection with therapy; it is a device that has been used to approach therapy, and it is not the only possible device. It is quite possible that, in many instances lawyers, for all their commitment to formality, could do more to further therapy for their clients than can the small, overworked social staffs of the courts…. (*In re Gault*, 1967; The President's Commission on Law Enforcement and the Administration of Justice, 1967).

This one court decision moved juvenile courts from informal—in some instances almost secretive—proceedings into more formalized, consistent processes. Besides introducing the important due process rights already accorded adults, the Gault decision transformed the juvenile court into a court in which judges and referees wore robes and sat behind high benches, but also one in which many children came to court with an attorney, and one in which prosecutors were assigned to attend all juvenile court hearings.

Both the Kent case and the Gault case were revolutionary for the juvenile court, but other rights for juveniles were established by subsequent court decisions. Those cases, and the rights that came about as a result, are featured below:

- *Tinker v. Des Moines Independent Community School District* (1969): The First Amendment applies to juveniles and protects their constitutional right to free speech.
- *In re Winship* (1970): Juveniles have a right to the criminal court standard of "beyond a reasonable doubt" where loss of freedom is a possible outcome.
- *McKeiver v. Pennsylvania* (1971): Juveniles have a right to a jury trial, but that right is not absolute.
- *Breed v. Jones* (1975): Double jeopardy exists if a juvenile is adjudicated as a delinquent in a juvenile court and, then, later, is tried for the same offense in a criminal court.
- *Fare v. Michael* (1979): The "totality of circumstances" standard applies for evaluating interrogation of juveniles by police without parents or attorneys present.
- *Eddings v. Oklahoma* (1982): The death penalty applies to juveniles and is not cruel or unusual punishment per se.
- *Schall v. Martin* (1984): Preventive detention of juveniles is constitutional.
- *Thompson v. Oklahoma* (1988): The death penalty applied to juveniles convicted of murder who are under the age of 16 at the time of the murder is cruel and unusual punishment.
- *Stanford v. Kentucky* (1989) and *Wilkins v. Missouri* (1989): The death penalty is not cruel and unusual punishment if the juvenile is 16 or 17 at the time the murder was committed.
- *Maryland v. Craig* (1990): Allows child abuse victims to testify on closed circuit television in a court trial.
- *Roper v. Simmons* (2005): The Supreme Court rules that the death penalty is prohibited in the case of juveniles who were under the age of 18 at the time they commited a capital crime.

Fundamental rights during juvenile proceedings

While the above bulleted list includes the most important U.S. Supreme Court decisions and the rights established in each, it is useful to take a closer look at some of the basic rights to which juveniles are entitled.

In the landmark case of *In re Gault* (1967), the Supreme Court declared that juveniles are entitled to an attorney only after adversarial proceedings have been started against them. However, while this has meant that many young people are represented by an attorney in juvenile court hearings, the reality that research has shown is that less than half of all minors appearing in juvenile courts have the advice of counsel (Taylor and Fritsch, 2011). The reason for this may vary from state to state; however, it could be that many parents are reluctant to retain an attorney, or it could be due to the inadequacy of public defender legal services in some areas.

When juvenile courts were first established, it was considered paramount that juvenile court proceedings be kept confidential and the names of minors appearing in juvenile courts be protected. Over the years, the U.S. Supreme Court has had to determine if juveniles are entitled to privacy and confidentiality in court proceedings. The rulings of the Supreme Court, along with state statutes and actual practices, establish the following:

- Despite state confidentiality laws, the probation status of a juvenile witness can be revealed during cross-examination in a trial.
- Despite state laws that make it illegal to publish the name of a juvenile charged with a crime, this is inconsistently practiced.
- Despite the Supreme Court ruling that keeping a juvenile's name confidential is unconstitutional, it has also allowed judges in juvenile proceedings to retain the right to determine if and when protecting the privacy of a minor during delinquency proceedings will serve the broader interest of furthering the juvenile's rehabilitation (Taylor and Fritsch, 2011).

As it turns out, a number of states, in the interest of holding young people accountable for their behavior, have passed laws allowing public access to juvenile proceedings. And the courts have allowed this. The courts have declared that there is no constitutional confidentiality right for an alleged or adjudicated delinquent. This also means that more and more states are allowing juvenile court hearings to be open to the public and the media—particularly if the case involves a serious offense or if the juvenile is a habitual offender.

Bail is a right that is granted by the Eighth Amendment to the Constitution of the United States. In practice, though, this is a qualified right. This means that it is up to a judge in adult criminal courts to determine if bail will be allowed, and the amount of that bail. When it comes to juveniles, they have not expressly been given the right to bail by the Supreme Court. In fact, the high court has ruled that juveniles may be held in preventive detention as protective custody. It is generally the case that if juveniles are taken into custody by the police, their parents are notified and the minor is released into a parent's custody. The same is true if a young person is taken to a detention facility—he or she will likely be released to the parents.

These days, several states authorize bail for juveniles in the state statutes. However, there are other states that specifically forbid the use of bail for juveniles.

It is well-known that adult defendants have a right to a trial by a jury of their peers. This is guaranteed by the Sixth Amendment. But does this constitutional right apply to juveniles?

In the U.S. Supreme Court decision in *McKeiver v. Pennsylvania* (1971), the court clearly denied juveniles the right to a jury trial in delinquency hearings. But the Supreme Court said in McKeiver that states are free to pass legislation allowing juveniles to have jury trials. Some states have, in fact, passed such laws granting juveniles the right to request a jury trial. For the most part, state juvenile courts will consider requests for a jury trial and may grant these requests under certain circumstances.

In the states that do allow jury trials in juvenile courts, the number of jurors, their functions, and the number of votes needed for adjudication vary (del Carmen and Trulson, 2006). Some states allow a majority vote by jurors, while others require unanimity for a verdict. Only four states (Alaska, Massachusetts, Michigan, and West Virginia) will consider a jury trial in all delinquency cases. Usually, jury trials will be considered—and at times granted—when the youth is charged with a serious offense.

It should be pointed out, however, that once a juvenile is waived to an adult court, trial by jury becomes an absolute constitutional right.

Can juvenile court hearings be appealed?

Juveniles do not have a constitutional right to an appeal of their adjudication or disposition. However, all states grant juveniles the right to appeal. Although, theoretically, the prosecutor has a right to appeal juvenile cases, this is rarely exercised (Bartollas and Miller, 2005).

FOR FURTHER LEARNING

Can juveniles knowingly and competently waive their rights?

Research by Thomas Grisso, PhD, professor of psychiatry, director of psychology, and director of the Law-Psychiatry Program at the University of Massachusetts Medical School, shows that juveniles have little grasp of their constitutional rights. He studied a large sample of juveniles and found that only 10% of them chose not to waive their rights in situations in which serious charges were alleged (Champion, 2010). Grisso found that juveniles demonstrated less comprehension than adults of their *Miranda* rights, had less understanding of the wording of the *Miranda warning*, misunderstood their right to counsel, and did not understand their right to remain silent (many believed they could later be punished if they failed to tell about their criminal activities) (Champion, 2010).

FOR FURTHER CONSIDERATION

Questions for discussion

1. Is there a compelling reason for allowing the public and the media to know the names of youth appearing in juvenile courts?
2. Should children and teens have jury trials or jury adjudications? Why or why not?

Review for chapter four

Important terms to know:

In re Gault: A landmark case decided by the U.S. Supreme Court in 1967, which provided more due process rights for juveniles.
Waiver hearing: A hearing in a juvenile court to decide if a juvenile should be transferred to an adult court for a trial.
Miranda rights: The rights accorded to criminal defendants by the U.S. Supreme Court in 1966, which allows individuals to remain silent and to be represented by counsel during police interrogations.

Study guide questions

Choose the right answers from the choices below.

1. In the case *Kent v. U.S.* (1966), the U.S. Supreme Court stated that counsel in a juvenile case must be provided meaningful information and that a juvenile was entitled to hearing
   a. To determine if they should be locked up
   b. To determine if they should be charged with a status offense
   c. To determine if they should be transferred to an adult criminal court
   d. To determine if they should be sent to a new school
2. In the case of *In re Gault* (1967), the U.S. Supreme Court ruled that juveniles were entitled to
   a. The same sentences as adults
   b. The important due process rights already accorded to adults
   c. The presence of a child psychologist during all hearings
   d. The serving of healthy food in juvenile detention
3. When juvenile courts were first established, it was considered paramount that juvenile court proceedings
   a. Be kept confidential
   b. Be open in revealing the names of minors to the press
   c. Be open to other children who knew the juvenile appearing in court
   d. Be televised
4. Although bail is a right that is granted by the Eighth Amendment to adults, the U.S. Supreme Court
   a. Has said that juveniles can't afford bail
   b. Has limited bail to a certain dollar amount for minors
   c. Has not expressly given the right to bail to juveniles
   d. Has indicated that parents can pay the bail for their minor children

chapter five

Who are the players in juvenile court hearings?

The major players in a juvenile court hearing are

- The judge or referee
- The juvenile
- The juvenile's parents or guardians
- The defense attorney
- The prosecutor
- The probation officer

Judge

The trend in the United States over the past decade or so has been a movement toward single trial courts. This means that often juvenile courts have become part of family courts or domestic relations courts. Judges, then, are usually elected to the trial court and then assigned to hear juvenile court or family court cases.

Juvenile court judges have an enormously important and difficult job. Since jury trials in juvenile courts rarely are allowed—as you just learned in chapter four—the judge is responsible for hearing the case and deciding the outcome of the case.

But judges are much more than just decision makers, who choose how to dispose of delinquency and neglect cases. In addition, they have to make certain that juveniles appearing in court receive the legal and constitutional rights to which they are entitled. They also have to ensure that the agencies or systems that detect, investigate, resolve, and bring cases to court are working fairly and efficiently. And, ultimately, they have to monitor the progress of the child, the family, and the other agencies or departments of the court to make sure that each complies with the terms of the court's orders.

Juvenile court judges have broad discretion in how they will conduct the business of the juvenile court. Some are formal and legalistic; some are informal and nonadversarial (Fuller, 2013). No matter their approach, they all must ensure that the best interests of the child are served—and guarded. This is particularly true if the parents are absent or in conflict with their child. In these kind of situations, the judge may appoint a *guardian ad litem* who can advocate for the child's best interests in the case.

It should also be emphasized that juvenile court and family court judges have a responsibility to continuously be aware of research pertaining to children and juvenile delinquency, and to avail themselves of continuing legal education. The National Council of Juvenile and Family Court Judges sponsors journals and educational programs for judges to help them stay informed and current.

Referee

Many juvenile courts employ referees who hear cases. In different states, referees go by different titles. In Michigan, they are called referees; in the state of Washington, they are called commissioners; In Maryland, they are referred to as masters. While judges are elected, referees are appointed.

Their roles, though, may also vary from state to state. In some states they essentially play a role similar to a judge, while in other states they may hear cases only at the fact-finding stage or only handle detention hearings. In general, though, the trend is for juvenile courts to rely more on referees because the caseload pressures make it impossible for judges to hear all of the cases.

Prosecutor

Prosecutors in juvenile courts are responsible for bringing cases to the court's attention. Although prosecutors—who in some jurisdictions are called district attorneys or state attorneys—do not work for the juvenile court, but are employed by the local prosecuting attorney or district attorney's office, they will typically be assigned to the juvenile court.

Prosecutors play a very important role in juvenile courts. It can be said that their decisions determine the juvenile court's caseload to a great extent. It is the prosecutor who makes decisions about which cases will result in a petition being sent to the juvenile court. In this role, the prosecutor can determine which particular juvenile case will be sent to the court and which will be disposed of without a formal adjudication hearing, through plea bargaining, diversion, or dismissal.

In larger courts—usually those in urban settings—prosecutors may be involved in juvenile cases at every step of the process—from writing a petition through disposition. Prosecutors, thus, may play a role in all pretrial motions, preliminary hearings, and consent decrees. They represent the local or state government in making sure that youthful offenders get the hearings or disposition they deserve.

As the state's—really the people's—representative, the prosecutor must consider his or her role in protecting the community from the danger of harmful conduct of the juvenile defendant, while, at the same time, balancing the youth's needs for rehabilitation. Essentially, the prosecutor tries to reconcile the complex and sometimes conflicting goals of making certain that the community is safe from a particular juvenile and, at the same time, promoting the best interests of that young person.

At one time, prosecutors played almost no role in juvenile court cases. With the important court decisions of the 1960s and the due process revolution, the prosecutors' part has been expanded so that they attend every juvenile court hearing. And since the groundbreaking court decisions established more due process rights for minors, prosecutors now must be more sensitive to those rights, ensuring that they are not violated.

You will recall that one of the early Supreme Court decisions was *In re Winship* (1970), in which the court ruled that the standard of proof in a juvenile justice case should be similar to that in an adult criminal case: beyond a reasonable doubt. The effect of this ruling was to make the prosecutor's job more difficult in juvenile cases. Even though most juvenile adjudication hearings are bench trials rather than jury trials, still it is incumbent on the prosecutor to prove to the judge or referee's satisfaction that the youth was guilty of an offense beyond a reasonable doubt.

Defense attorney

In the Gault decision in 1967, the Supreme Court made it very clear that a juvenile accused of committing a crime had the right to counsel. Since that decision, defense attorneys have been more common in juvenile courts.

With more defense attorneys appearing in juvenile courts, the American Bar Association has recommended that juveniles be provided with quality legal representation (Vito and Simonsen, 2004). Defense attorneys must perform a number of critical tasks, including gathering information regarding the juvenile's history, family, education, and community ties, in order to assist the court in making an appropriate disposition. Furthermore, collecting such information and sharing it with the court helps in preventing unnecessary pretrial detention, helps avoid unnecessary transfer to adult courts, and ensures that dispositions are suitable for each child or adolescent they represent. Just as the prosecutor represents the state, the defense attorney represents the juvenile, and both protect their client at every stage of the proceeding.

With the increasing frequency of defense attorneys in juvenile courts, it is also commonplace for courts to appoint public defenders for indigent juveniles. Every juvenile court provides public defenders for minors and their families when they cannot afford to retain private counsel. Lawyers appointed by the state may be private lawyers who are appointed as part of a court rotation system, or they may be public defenders. Public defenders are full-time state employees who represent the interests of those who cannot afford private counsel. Typically, public defenders work under heavy caseloads and have little support staff (Fuller, 2013). Also, public defenders don't have the resources to prepare for and participate in many hearings and, therefore, may encourage their clients to plead guilty.

Critics of the idea of bringing more attorneys into the juvenile court process believe that although the stated purpose of counsel is to ensure that the constitutional rights of juveniles are protected, they also fear that, with attorney involvement, the proceedings become more formal and that juveniles may actually receive less fair treatment (Office of Juvenile Justice and Delinquency Prevention, 2007). Nonetheless, for especially serious cases, defense attorneys are increasingly found to be useful and necessary to safeguard juvenile rights, while holding the juvenile justice system more accountable regarding the treatment of juvenile offenders.

The dark secret of juvenile courts, as University of Minnesota law professor Barry Feld describes it, is that counsel is routinely waived by juveniles and their families (Jackson and Knepper, 2003). The findings of research in Minnesota has found that less than half of juveniles adjudicated delinquent received the assistance of counsel; one-third of juveniles removed from their homes and a quarter of those placed in secure detention were not represented by an attorney (Feld, 1989).

Juvenile defendant

As is obvious, a key player is the juvenile. Most judges and referees will give juveniles the opportunity to speak in court to defend themselves, or to talk about mitigating circumstances related to the offense. How the juvenile presents himself or herself in terms of language, dress, attitude, and behavior, may play an influential part in both adjudication and disposition.

Parents

In most instances, a juvenile delinquency or neglect hearing cannot proceed without the presence of the parents or guardians of the child. The juvenile court is obligated to provide the parents with timely notice of any and all hearings, and to make every effort to ensure they attend hearings. Their input during hearings, particularly in detention, intake, and adjudication hearings, is important—often critical.

Probation officer or court caseworker

Although, in the early stages of court proceedings, court staff—other than the judge or referee—will not be present, that changes in subsequent hearings.

In an adjudication hearing, for instance, a probation officer or court caseworker may be present to submit a written report or to testify in regards to their social history or pretrial investigation report. This suggests the sometimes complex role played by probation officers, who may be assigned to a juvenile after he or she has been scheduled for an adjudication hearing.

The duty of the probation officer, who, in some courts, will have other titles, such as court worker or court caseworker, is to conduct an interview with the juvenile and his or her parents or guardians to learn more about the child's background and current life. Sometimes referred to as an investigation report, the caseworker's job is to investigate the social, legal, emotional, and educational history of the child in order to learn as much as possible about the child's life up to the court hearing. Such reports may detail a child's physical or medical background, educational history, psychological problems, and family relationships. The conclusion of this report will, typically, be a set of recommendations to the court. This report aids the judge or referee in better understanding the child and the family so that decisions made in hearings will be individually tailored for that particular individual.

In later hearings, such as a review hearing or a violation of probation hearing, the youth's probation officer will be in a position to testify about the juvenile's actual experiences in treatment and on probation. Often, the same probation officer or caseworker who did the initial presentence investigation and report will have served as the probation officer after disposition, and will have become familiar with the child and his or her family.

Key players

Although the key players in the juvenile court represent varying interests, they must all find a way of working together to achieve the goals of ensuring justice, providing for the best interest of minors, and moving a large number of cases through what is—in many jurisdictions—a heavily-burdened system. Juvenile courts tend to be far less adversarial than other courts, but each player brings his or her own viewpoints and attitude to the juvenile justice process. Because of the varied players' backgrounds, training, and views of juvenile delinquency, abuse, or neglect, they may have vastly different views as to how a child and society will best be served in the juvenile court.

LEARNING MORE

Few judges come to the bench with a background or interest in juvenile law. Many judges spend a short period of time in the juvenile court and then rotate into a criminal court judgeship. Attracting competent judges to the juvenile court bench is one of the most serious problems facing the juvenile court system (Jackson and Knepper, 2003).

Judges may avoid juvenile court for various reasons. The juvenile court may be regarded, substantively, more as a social rather than a legal institution. As a result, juvenile court dockets may possess low status within the legal community. Furthermore, juvenile law may be held in low esteem by bar associations. That may be true in law schools as well, where other kinds of law—criminal law and finance law, for instance—are held in higher regard than the practice of law dealing with issues related to the family, domestic relations, delinquency, and neglect. Law school curriculums may have few courses in juvenile law. However, there are a few law schools, such as Loyola Law School in Los Angeles, that have a concentration in juvenile and family law. Loyola Law School in Los Angeles has a Juvenile Justice Clinic, which allows law students the opportunity to represent juveniles in juvenile court proceedings.

FOR FURTHER CONSIDERATION

Questions for discussion

1. Why is it difficult for the key players to agree on how a particular youth should be handled by the juvenile court?
2. What are the reasons why a judge might opt for a judgeship in an adult criminal court rather than a juvenile court?

Review for chapter five

Important terms to know:

Juvenile court judges: Juvenile court judges are elected officials who are generally responsible for hearing juvenile cases and deciding outcomes of those cases.

Guardian ad litem: An individual appointed by the court who can advocate for the child's best interests in a juvenile court case.

Referees: Although they go by different names in different states, referees are appointed, and they essentially play a role similar to that of a judge in a juvenile court.

Public defenders: Public defenders are attorneys and often full-time state employees who represent the interests of those who cannot afford private counsel.

Social history or investigation report: In many juvenile courts, the job of the probation officer or the court caseworker is to investigate the social, legal, emotional, and educational history of the child in order to learn as much as possible about the child's life up to the court hearing and provide a report to the judge or referee.

Study guide questions

Choose the right answers from the choices below.

1. It is the prosecutor assigned to the juvenile court who makes decisions about
   a. Which cases will be placed in detention or on probation.
   b. Which cases will appear before a judge or referee.
   c. Which cases will result in a petition being sent to the juvenile court.
   d. Which cases will appear in court without a parent present.

2. As the state's representative, the prosecutor must consider his or her role in protecting the community from the danger of harmful conduct of the juvenile defendant, while at the same time
   a. Deciding what punishment is appropriate.
   b. Balancing the youth's needs for rehabilitation.
   c. Selecting the treatment agency for the child.
   d. Being as tough as possible.

3. Every juvenile court provides public defenders for minors and their families when
   a. They cannot afford to retain private counsel.
   b. They have a high level of income.
   c. The family pleads poverty.
   d. The child thinks it would be cool to have his or her own attorney.

4. The dark secret of juvenile courts, as University of Minnesota law professor Barry Feld describes it, is that counsel
   a. Is routinely unavailable to meet with the youth and his or her family.
   b. Usually don't have a law degree.
   c. Is frequently too busy to defend a juvenile offender.
   d. Is routinely waived by juveniles and their families.

5. Attracting competent judges to the juvenile court bench is
   a. One of the most serious problems facing the juvenile court.
   b. Very easily accomplished, because the juvenile court job is easy.
   c. Difficult, because most judges hate kids.
   d. A problem, because judges earn less as juvenile court judges.

chapter six

The first step
Intake hearings

Intake is the first step—the initial phase—of the juvenile court process. Intake is the stage at which someone decides whether a petition that has been received by the court merits formal court action.

According to Griffin and Torbet:

> Intake may be the most crucial case processing point in the juvenile justice system because so much follows from that decision. Intake authority is entrusted to prosecutors in some jurisdictions—either in all cases or in those involving allegations of serious crimes—and to juvenile court intake or juvenile probation departments in others (Griffin and Torbet, 2002, p. 34).

The intake officer—sometimes referred to as the intake referee in some courts—decides whether a case should move ahead for court processing. The intake officer or intake referee can decide to recommend that the petition be filed and that a next hearing, often an initial hearing, be scheduled. However, the intake officer has the discretion to release the youth with a warning or a reprimand, release the youth with the stipulation that he or she enrolls in a community diversion program, or be placed on consent probation. In addition, the intake officer can determine that the juvenile be detained pending further court action or simply, as happens in most instances, be released to the custody of his or her parents. If the child is detained, this will result in a detention hearing.

At the intake stage, the hearing is not held to determine whether the juvenile is guilty of the offense contained in the petition, but to decide if the matter deserves or requires the court's attention. A later hearing will decide adjudication—that is, guilt or innocence. Essentially, the intake hearing officer must ask two basic questions:

1. Is the petition or complaint against the juvenile legally sufficient to proceed with further court actions?
2. Does a hearing with the juvenile and his or her parents (or guardians) indicate that the case should be formally processed?

If the intake officer answers both questions in the affirmative, then the case is referred to the juvenile court for official processing (Hess, 2010).

Assessment

Another function of the intake officer is to decide if a formal assessment or evaluation of the juvenile should take place before future hearings take place. That might mean a referral for a psychological or psychiatric assessment of the youngster. Some juvenile courts have their own assessment center or psychological clinic, and a referral can take place immediately after the intake hearing. Other courts may not have an assessment center, but they may contract with private psychological and psychiatric clinics for court-ordered evaluations. Often, a mental health evaluation is an important step in assessing juvenile offenders, because such an evaluation can assist in determining the most effective disposition for that minor.

Consent decrees

One function of the intake officer, as indicated above, is to decide if the youth can be handled short of official juvenile court involvement. While diversion to a community treatment program is one option, so is a consent decree—sometimes referred to as informal probation. The intake officer can enter into an informal agreement with the juvenile and his or her parents, which will mean that the child will not be scheduled for further court processing at this time but agree to the consent decree or consent docket for unofficial handling. This means that if the juvenile agrees to and completes conditions imposed by the intake officer—which could include such conditions as a curfew, regular school attendance, restitution, or counseling—his or her involvement with the court would be terminated without a court record. If the juvenile does not complete the agreed-upon conditions, the intake officer could then authorize formal court action.

JUVENILE JUSTICE FACTS

Between 1985 and 2009, the likelihood that a delinquency case would be handled informally (without filing a petition for adjudication) decreased. While the overall delinquency caseload in juvenile courts increased 30% between 1985 and 2009, the number of nonpetitioned cases increased 9% and the number of petitioned cases increased 54%.

The overall likelihood of formal handling was greater for more serious offenses within the same general offense category. In 2009, for example, 71% of aggravated assault cases were handled formally, compared with 51% of simple assault cases. Similarly, 75% of burglary cases and 78% of motor vehicle theft cases were handled formally by juvenile courts, compared with 40% of larceny–theft and 43% of trespassing cases.

Youth younger than 16 accounted for 49% of the delinquency cases handled formally by juvenile courts in 2009; females accounted for 23% and white youth accounted for 60% of petitioned cases.

Between 1985 and 2009, the likelihood of formal processing increased from 43% to 54% for drug offense cases, from 48% to 57% for public order cases, from 44% to 51% for property offense cases, and from 55% to 58% for person offense cases (Puzzenchara et al., 2012).

preliminary hearings. But the court has indicated that these stages of the process are critical stages, because incriminating evidence could be obtained that might be used against them later. But the question is this: Is intake a critical stage?

While the U.S. Supreme Court has not addressed that issue, a New York court has. In the case of *In re Frank H.* (1972), a New York court held that juveniles do not have a constitutional right to counsel at intake because it is not a "critical stage" (del Carmen and Trulson, 2006). The court concluded that intake was not a critical stage because New York law prohibits the use of information gathered at intake to be used in a guilt-finding proceeding (an adjudication hearing), and because the purpose of intake is to gather relevant information to help the juvenile (del Carmen and Trulson, 2006). Despite this finding, some states do allow for juveniles to be represented at intake by counsel.

In Sections III, IV, and V, you will learn more about specific kinds of hearings, the options that judges and referees have at those hearings, and you will be presented many cases for your consideration. You will have a chance to play the role of a judge or referee to decide what should be recommended in every case to help in the rehabilitation of each juvenile you will learn about. In chapter seven, you will have the chance to be an intake officer to decide how two juveniles, Brody and Makayla, should be handled. In other words, you will make the call to determine how they should be dealt with by the juvenile court.

A juvenile's legal rights at intake

Before an intake officer can make a decision about whether to dismiss, handle informally, or proceed with a formal court hearing, the juvenile must meet at an intake hearing. At an intake hearing, or intake conference, as they are sometimes called, the intake officer may ask questions that tend to incriminate the juvenile. For example, the intake officer may ask about the alleged offense, whether the juvenile is responsible, and such other questions as prior offenses, the location of missing property, or the use of a weapon during the offense.

This is particularly important for the juvenile, because, in order to be offered an informal disposition, he or she will have to admit responsibility for the alleged delinquent act (del Carmen and Trulson, 2006). So, it is important for juveniles to know whether they have any procedural protections, such as the right to an attorney or the right to remain silent, during the intake process.

Although juveniles do have certain rights before adjudication, they may not have them during the intake process. Certainly, the U.S. Supreme Court has determined that juveniles have the right to counsel during preindictment custodial interrogation and during

LEARNING MORE

Diversion is a process whereby a child is referred to a program for counseling, or treatment of some form, in lieu of referral to the juvenile court. The President's Commission of Law Enforcement and Administration of Justice describes diversion as a process of referring youths to an existing community treatment program instead of further juvenile justice processing (Houston and Barton, 2005).

Diversion is designed to suspend or terminate juvenile justice processing of a young person in favor of release or referral to alternate services. To many, diversion means referral to programs outside the justice system, say, to a boys' or girls' club or to a family counseling agency. But diversion is controversial because some critics of the practice fear that it will produce a net widening of the juvenile justice apparatus. What this means is that diversion might be used as a kind of unofficial disposition for youths who would otherwise be screened out of the system (Houston and Barton, 2005).

Nonetheless, diversion is widely practiced, and is frequently used by the police, prosecutors, and juvenile court intake departments.

FOR FURTHER CONSIDERATION

Questions for discussion

1. Is the intake hearing really the most crucial step in the juvenile justice process? Why or why not might this be true?
2. How is diversion a net-widening process? What are the pros and cons of diversion for minors?

Review for chapter six

Important terms to know:

Intake hearing: A hearing in a juvenile court to determine if the case deserves a formal court hearing.
Consent docket: An unofficial way of handling a minor, short of official juvenile court action.
Diversion: Instead of a formal juvenile court hearing and potential designation as a delinquent, a juvenile is referred for services outside of the justice system.
Net-widening: Instead of dismissing minors entirely from the system, unofficial and informal dispositions may mean that youth are still part of the justice system.

Study guide questions

Choose the right answers from the choices below.

1. At the intake stage, the hearing is not held to determine whether the juvenile is guilty of the offense contained in the petition, but to decide
   a. If the youth has a bad family life
   b. If the case deserves to go on to an adult criminal court
   c. If the matter deserves or requires the court's attention
   d. If the youth should be considered dangerous
2. One of the most essential questions to be answered in the intake hearing is
   a. Should the juvenile be found guilty of a crime?
   b. Does a hearing with the juvenile produce a good feeling for everyone concerned?
   c. Does a hearing with the juvenile and his or her parents indicate that the case should be formally processed?
   d. Does the child feel guilty for what he or she did?
3. The child and the family at the intake hearing could agree to the consent decree or consent docket for unofficial handling. This means that if the juvenile agrees to and completes conditions imposed by the intake officer
   a. His or her involvement with the court would be terminated without a court record
   b. His or her involvement with the court would result in a lesser sentence
   c. His or her conditions of probation would be less severe
   d. His or her conditions would earn him or her a financial reward
4. Between 1985 and 2009, the likelihood that a delinquency case would be handled informally (without filing a petition for adjudication)
   a. Increased dramatically
   b. Increased slightly
   c. Decreased dramatically
   d. Decreased
5. A New York court decided, in the case of *In re Frank H.* (1972), that juveniles do not have a constitutional right to counsel at intake because it is
   a. Too soon
   b. A bad time for parents
   c. Just an informal procedure
   d. Not a critical stage

section three

You make the call in juvenile court hearings

chapter seven

Decisions at intake

Introducing the intake referee

The process by which juveniles reach the juvenile court begins with a petition. In the adult system, this is referred to as the complaint; in juvenile courts, it's called the petition. Petitions come from the police, the school, the prosecutor, or a parent. It tells the court what this juvenile did wrong and it asks the court to take jurisdiction over this child.

When a petition is received by the court, it goes to the *intake department* and is assigned to an intake referee. The intake referee is an attorney whose job is to hold intake hearings and decide a proper course of action for the petition, based on the procedures outlined in the juvenile code for that state.

Intake may be described as a "weeding-out" process (del Carmen and Trulson, 2006). The intake referee conducts a "preliminary inquiry" to determine which cases will be handled with a formal adjudication hearing and which cases will be resolved informally. If the juvenile has been detained, this first event is called a preliminary hearing. The preliminary hearing must begin within 24 hours of the juvenile's detention. In general, it may be said that the delinquency cases requiring formal court processing are those that are more serious or more frequent, and those in which most other options have been exhausted.

Some of the factors that intake officers may take into consideration, in trying to determine the best method of resolving a case are

- The seriousness of the offense
- The juvenile's prior record or previous contacts with the juvenile justice system, including the police
- The juvenile's conduct or behavior problems at home or at school
- The age, maturity, and attitude of the juvenile
- The ability of the parents to control the juvenile
- The information provided by the victim

The options available to the intake referee

At a preliminary inquiry or a preliminary hearing, the intake referee has these options:

- Dismiss the petition and send the child home
- Authorize the petition for a formal juvenile court hearing
- Place the child on the consent docket
- Authorize the petition for a formal juvenile court hearing and, in addition, detain the child in a detention center pending his or her hearing
- Refer the juvenile and his family to an outside agency for non-court services. This process is called *diversion*

The consent docket

The *consent docket*—also known as the "consent decree" and the "consent probation"—is an option that can be exercised at intake. It is an unofficial type of probation. The intake hearing officer, with the consent of the juvenile and his or her family, will make an agreement that the youth will not be scheduled for a juvenile court hearing—at least not at this time. Instead, he or she will be placed on the consent docket, which essentially means they are on unofficial probation until a future review date. At that time, say, six months in the future, the juvenile and the family will return and the child's behavior during the interim will be reviewed. The intake referee may have also assigned the child or the family to complete certain tasks (attend counseling, make restitution to a victim, take drug screens, attend a jail program, write an essay, or attend school regularly, for instance). If those required tasks have been successfully completed, the referee will close the case without authorizing the petition. The juvenile is, then, released.

One benefit of the consent docket or consent probation is that the young person does not have a juvenile court record. However, if the child has not been successful in meeting the requirements of the intake officer, he or she now may be scheduled for a formal juvenile court hearing. The prosecutor's office must also agree that the court can use the consent docket for petitions it files.

You make the call in these intake hearing cases

Having learned more about what constitutes an intake hearing and the options available to the intake officer, now it is your turn to consider two cases of juveniles who were referred to juvenile courts on petitions alleging delinquent offenses. Decide how you would handle these cases if you were the intake referee. Consider the facts in each case and decide what you would do. Write your decision in the space following each case. Be prepared to state your rationale for your decision and be ready to defend your decision.

The case of Brody, age 15

Brody is 15 years old and in the 10th grade at a special school for the emotionally impaired. He has been certified as emotionally impaired since elementary school, and has received extensive inpatient and outpatient mental health services for years. He is currently prescribed the psychiatric drugs Wellbutrin and Seroquel. The daily doses of these drugs are closely monitored and adjusted when necessary by the psychiatrist who prescribed them.

Brody is a somewhat introverted boy who is small for his age and has a slight build. He is only 5'3" tall and weighs just 120 pounds. He has been the target of significant bullying since moving to his present school district when he was in middle school. He has endured multiple, mean-spirited attacks, which has forced him to seek help from teachers, counselors, and administrators several times. However, the ridicule and teasing by his peers have not stopped. At one point in the past year, it grew so extreme that police intervention was required.

Brody is appearing in front of the intake referee on one count of arson. He admits throwing lit matches into two garbage cans and a recycling bin at school. He denies that his actions were directly connected to the bullying, but it certainly appears to have been an attempt to gain attention or, perhaps, the arson might even have been some sort of revenge. Neither he, nor his mother and father, who both accompanied him to this intake hearing, believe that the bullying or teasing justifies setting fires at school. Brody indicates regret during the hearing. He describes his actions as foolish and states that it will not happen again.

While it appears to the intake referee that he feels sorry for his actions, the referee also wonders if Brody fully understands the seriousness of his actions and the potential

he created for greater loss and damage. When asked why he shouldn't have thrown matches into the garbage cans and recycling bins, Brody replies, "You shouldn't start fires." When the referee asks, "Why not?" Brody's answer is: "It is wrong." Maybe, the referee thinks, his lack of insight could be related to his mental health issues and emotional deficiencies.

Brody's ongoing mental health treatment appears to be most critical at this time. His parents point out that, since the arson occurred, some positive changes have taken place. He was recently placed in his current high school, which is a more appropriate school for Brody, as it is designed for youth with special needs. It has a low student-to-staff ratio, and the teachers are extremely involved with each student. He now has a school counselor that he really likes and feels comfortable opening up to. His teacher is also very supportive. His community-based counselor and his therapist know him well and see him often. Recently, he has been more open and engaged at home. His parents think he is currently on a positive path, and they point out that he seems to be building a more solid sense of who he is and is showing signs of being more self-confident.

YOU MAKE THE CALL

Now it's your turn to make the call. As the intake referee, what would you decide to do with Brody? Write your decision in the space below.

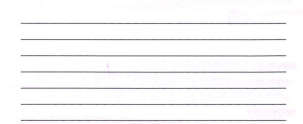

_____
_____
_____
_____
_____
_____
_____

After you have made the call, feel free to go to the appendix and review the decision of the actual intake referee in this case. Compare your decision with his and review the rationale for the referee's decision. Then check out the follow-up. What happened to Brody in the year following this intake hearing?

_____
_____
_____

JUVENILE JUSTICE FACT

According to the Office of Juvenile Justice and Delinquency Prevention, in 2011 law enforcement agencies in the U.S. arrested 1,470,000 juveniles under the age of 18. This number was 7% lower than 2010 and 31% fewer than the number of arrests in 2002.

The case of Makayla, age 13

Makayla is 13 years old and in the 8th grade in a rural middle school. She lives with her mother, and her parents were divorced when Makayla was 9 years old. Her father sees her about one weekend a month. Makayla is an only child.

Makayla was arrested by the police at her home when she and her mother got into a physical fight and her mother was cut by flying glass. She was taken to the county detention center and charged with domestic violence. The next day, she pleaded guilty to the charge. Her mother said she did not feel safe letting her come home.

At the hearing in front of the intake referee, she pleads guilty to the charge, but significantly minimizes the offense by stating that she threw a vase at the ground and the shards of glass only hit her mother by chance. She denies any intent to hurt or cut her mother. Listening to Makayla and her mother talking at the hearing, the intake referee thinks the matter appears to be more of a home incorrigibility case that escalated into an altercation between Makayla and her mother—and that resulted in police intervention.

Both Makayla and her mother admit to problems over the past two to three years. She has not done well at school, where she has some below average grades, and has been sent to the office for talking back to teachers several times. Makayla identifies her parents' divorce four years ago as the beginning of her problems. She also points out that she and her mother moved from one city to another following the divorce, and in the new school district her attitudes, behavior, and choice in friends began to change. In the last few months, she has been associating with an older, negative peer group, leaving home without permission, and admits to experimenting with marijuana, although not in the past several weeks.

Her mother says that Makayla is often rude, disrespectful, and hurtful toward her mother, and she frequently disobeys basic home rules. She has been detained in secure detention at the county detention center for two weeks, and says she has not liked living there. She and her mother have had several positive visits during those two weeks, in which they speak about her past behaviors and how she will act differently when she returns home.

Makayla has been seeing a psychologist over the past year and plans to return to counseling when she goes home. Both she and her mother agree that it would probably be a good idea for her mother to become more involved in therapy too.

Despite minimizing her domestic violence crime, Makayla takes responsibility for a variety of poor behaviors and she seems to recognize that she needs to make changes to be successful at home.

The intake referee is considering the consent docket, however, and she thinks that several probationary requirements would be needed to help her make a successful transition back into her home.

YOU MAKE THE CALL

As the intake referee, what would you decide to do with Makayla? Write your decision in the space below.

_____
_____
_____
_____
_____
_____
_____

After you have made the call, feel free to go to the appendix and review the decision of the actual intake referee in this case. Compare your decision with hers and review the rationale for the referee's decision. Then check out the follow-up. What happened to Makayla in the year following this intake hearing?

_____
_____
_____

LEARNING MORE

Even before the establishment of the first juvenile court in Illinois in 1899, there were laws and ordinances in some cities and states that allowed for courts to take jurisdiction over incorrigible youth. That is still a possibility today. But there are basically three parts to the definition of incorrigibility. To be incorrigible, a child's actions must occur repeatedly and be disruptive, dangerous, disobedient, and in direct violation of lawful commands. One or two instances of disobedience could just be a part of growing up or being a teenager. Repeated, regularly occurring acts of disobedience may constitute a real problem.

Furthermore, the child's actions must also threaten the welfare, order, and/or safety of the environment and those near the child. Disorderly conduct in school, as well as drug or alcohol use, would fall into this category.

Finally, the orders that the child is violating must be legal commands. A child cannot be found incorrigible for disobeying illegal orders such as those that force the child to commit a crime or submit to being abused or hurt. Commands that violate the child's rights, such as his or her religious freedom, are also unlawful.

JUVENILE COURT STATISTICS

In 1999, approximately 17% of all referred cases to juvenile courts were dismissed by intake officers. Typically, intake officers will dismiss a case at the intake stage where there is insufficient evidence to support the allegations against the juvenile.

FOR FURTHER CONSIDERATION

Questions for discussion

1. What are the pros and cons of the consent docket?
2. What are some of the difficulties of being an intake referee?

Review for chapter seven

Important terms to know:

Preliminary inquiry: The intake referee conducts a "preliminary inquiry" to determine which cases will be handled with a formal adjudication hearing and which cases will be resolved informally.
Consent probation: Another term for the consent docket.

Study guide questions

Choose the right answers from the choices below.

1. When a petition is received by the court, it goes to the intake department and is assigned to
   a. A judge
   b. A guardian *ad litem*
   c. A probation officer
   d. An intake referee
2. The intake referee is an attorney whose job is to hold intake hearings and decide
   a. A proper course of action for the petition
   b. Whether the juvenile is sorry for his actions
   c. If restitution should be ordered
   d. A proper list of rules for the juvenile's home
3. One of the factors that an intake officer might take into consideration in trying to determine the best method of resolving a case is
   a. The juvenile's attitudes toward the juvenile court
   b. The juvenile's prior record or previous contacts with the police
   c. The behavior problems the child had as a preschooler
   d. The extent of the victim's injuries
4. According to the Office of Juvenile Justice and Delinquency Prevention, in 2011, law enforcement agencies in the United States arrested
   a. 55,000 juveniles under the age of 10
   b. 1,470,000 juveniles under the age of 18
   c. 2,200,000 juveniles accused of murder
   d. 7500 juveniles over the age of 18
5. An incorrigible child is one whose actions must
   a. Be one or two instances of disobeying his or her parents
   b. Occur repeatedly and be disruptive, dangerous, disobedient, and in direct violation of lawful commands
   c. Give his or her parents heartaches
   d. Be mildly offensive

chapter eight

Initial hearings

The initial hearing

If the referee authorizes a petition after a preliminary inquiry or intake hearing, the next step in the process is an *initial hearing*. Unless the juvenile has been detained, the initial hearing is a juvenile's first appearance in court. At the initial hearing, the judge or referee will appoint counsel for the child or teen if this is needed or requested, and will advise the minor and his or her parents of the charges, and of their rights in a juvenile proceeding.

If the juvenile admits the allegations of the delinquency petition at this initial hearing, the court could proceed immediately with a *dispositional hearing*, particularly if the child, his or her parents, and the prosecuting attorney (representing the state) agrees. Most typically, the dispositional hearing is scheduled for a future date. If the juvenile denies guilt, an *adjudication hearing* (or trial) is scheduled.

Juvenile detention

Juvenile detention centers are the equivalent of jails in the adult justice system. Detention centers, which often are operated by the county juvenile court, function as holding centers. Although detention centers hold juveniles at several points in the juvenile justice process, typically, they hold youth after they have been taken into custody and before the adjudication.

Although the purpose of juvenile detention centers is to ensure a young person's appearance in court, detention centers are also used to prevent further offenses by the juvenile while awaiting an adjudication hearing. They are used to ensure the safety of a juvenile who may pose a threat to himself or herself and others.

Once juveniles have been taken into custody by police officers, they may be taken with the court's permission to a detention center. The court then conducts a preliminary hearing. This is not the same as an initial hearing. Preliminary hearings are held within 24 h after the juvenile is taken into custody, and decisions are made as to whether the petition will be authorized, and whether the young person will be detained or released prior to the initial hearing. The juvenile may be released to the custody of his or her parents or guardians, with

or without conditions. In order to detain the juvenile beyond the 24-h period, some state laws require the court to find that there is probable cause to believe that the juvenile committed the alleged offense.

The hearing officer—either a juvenile court judge or referee—in a detention hearing must evaluate whether there is a "need" for detention. While probable cause is necessary to detain a juvenile, it is not always sufficient to keep a minor detained (del Carmen and Trulson, 2006).

Factors the hearing officer may consider for continued detention include

- The juvenile's family ties and relationships
- The juvenile's prior delinquency record
- The juvenile's record of appearances or nonappearances at court proceedings
- The violent nature of the alleged offense
- The juvenile's prior history of committing acts that resulted in bodily injury to others
- The juvenile's character and mental condition
- The court's ability to supervise the juvenile if placed with a parent or relative
- Any other factor indicating the juvenile's ties to the community, the risk of nonappearance, and the danger to the juvenile or the public if the youth is released

The options available to the judge or referee in a preliminary hearing

The judge or the referee holding the preliminary hearing has these options:

- Dismiss the petition and send the juvenile home
- Authorize the petition for a regular juvenile court hearing
- Maintain the juvenile in detention until the next hearing
- Release the juvenile to his or her parents or guardians
- Place the juvenile on the consent docket
- Refer the juvenile to alternative services under the provision that allows juvenile courts to do so

COURT DECISION AFFECTING JUVENILES

The U.S. Supreme Court ruled in *Schall v. Martin* (1984) that a juvenile could be held in preventive detention. The case originated with Gregory Martin, aged 14, who was arrested in 1977 and charged with robbery, assault, and possession of a weapon. He and two other youths allegedly hit a boy on the head with a loaded gun and stole his jacket and sneakers.

Gregory was held pending adjudication because the court found there was a "serious risk" that he would commit another crime if released. His attorney filed a *habeas corpus* action challenging the fundamental fairness of preventive detention. The lower appellate court reversed the juvenile court's detention order, arguing in part that pretrial detention is essentially punishment because many juveniles detained before trial are released before, or immediately after, adjudication.

However, the U.S. Supreme Court upheld the constitutionality of the preventive detention statute. The Supreme Court stated that preventive detention serves a legitimate state objective in protecting both the juvenile and society from pretrial crime, and is not intended to punish the juvenile. The Supreme Court found that there were enough procedures in place to protect juveniles from wrongful deprivation of liberty. The protections were provided by notice, a statement of the facts and reasons for detention, and a probable cause hearing within a short time. The Supreme Court also reasserted the *parens patriae* interests of the state in promoting the welfare of children.

You make the call in these preliminary hearing cases

After gaining a better understanding of preliminary hearings or detention hearings, you are now given the opportunity of reading about two different cases of young people who were taken into custody by the police and detained at detention centers. It is up to you—as the judge or referee in each case—to determine if they should be released or whether they should continue to be detained until their next juvenile court hearing. Decide how you would handle these cases if you were the referee or the judge. Consider the facts in each case and decide what you would do. Write your decision in the space following each case. Be prepared to state your rationale for your decision and be ready to defend your decision.

The case of Jamie, age 13

Jamie is a 13-year-old girl who lives with her mother and 7-year-old brother. Jamie's mother and father were never married and never lived together. Jamie sees her father regularly as he stops by their apartment to visit frequently. Her father is 39 years old, and works as a construction laborer. He has been in jail on two occasions, for assault and battery, and he has a history of alcoholism. Her mother is 38 years of age and has not worked for more than a year. She has worked in housekeeping at local hospitals in the past. She spent time in jail before Jamie was born for retail fraud. She denies any substance abuse problems. She describes the family financial situation as "poor."

Jamie is in the 6th grade at a middle school. She says that she doesn't like her school and says the girls there gossip too much. Her grades are average and lower than average. She has been suspended for fighting about four times in the past three years. Jamie contends it's not her fault that she has problems at school. She says that "the girls don't like me" and "the principal is just messing with me." Her mother says that Jamie has "an attitude" and "a mouth." She is argumentative at home and doesn't like to follow the rules.

Jamie was involved in retail fraud. She and several friends were in a T.J. Maxx store and stole several items, including socks, underwear, and t-shirts. When they were caught by store security, Jamie was belligerent and rude. The police were called when Jamie refused to give her name or address. She continued to be disrespectful toward the police after they arrived and was ultimately transported to the county juvenile detention center. Once there, she gave her name and her mother's phone number. This is Jamie's first police contact. She now says that she wishes she had never stolen from the store.

YOU MAKE THE CALL

Now you make the call. As the hearing officer, what would you decide to do with Jamie? Should she be released to her mother or held until her juvenile court hearing? Write your decision in the space below.

_____
_____
_____
_____
_____
_____
_____

After you have made your call, feel free to go to the appendix and review the decision of the actual court hearing officer in this case. Compare your decision with his and review the rationale for the referee's decision. Then check out the follow-up. What happened to Jamie in the year following this detention hearing?

_____
_____
_____

JUVENILE JUSTICE FACT

The Office of Juvenile Justice and Delinquency Prevention reports that, as of 2011, there were 61,400 juveniles detained in detention facilities in the United States: 86% were males and 14% were females.

The case of David, age 16

David is 16 years old and in the 11th grade at a local charter academy. He will turn 17 within weeks and will then be considered as an adult within the legal system. David resides with his single mother and his 9-year-old brother. David rarely sees his father, who has served repeated prison terms for various weapon and drug offenses.

David is in trouble with the court for the second time. He has been returned on a weapons offense within two weeks of being dismissed from a year-long probation order for a similar crime. Once again, he was in possession of a loaded gun and ran from the police when they arrived on the scene. When arrested he was transported by the police to the county detention facility.

Although David is now remorseful, there are great concerns regarding his impulsive decision making and extremely dangerous and reckless behavior. His actions put the safety of the community, police officers, and himself at great risk. There is also concern regarding the negative influence on his younger brother.

On the positive side, David has notable family support. He is enrolled in a good school, had been participating in counseling, and working at a fast-food restaurant. He has thought about his goals and plans to pursue a college degree.

Because David is almost 17, this is likely the last opportunity for the Juvenile Court to intervene and make efforts toward treatment and rehabilitation.

YOU MAKE THE CALL

As the hearing officer, what would you decide to do with David? Write your decision in the space below.

_____
_____
_____
_____
_____
_____

After you have made the call, feel free to go to the appendix and review the decision of the actual hearing officer in this case. Compare your decision with his, review the rationale for the hearing officer's decision. Then check out the follow-up. What happened to David in the year following this hearing?

_____
_____
_____

JUVENILE JUSTICE STATISTICS

The Office of Juvenile Justice and Delinquency Prevention statistics show that among detained juveniles (those awaiting adjudication, disposition, or placement elsewhere), 72% had been in the facility for at least a week, 52% for at least 15 days, and 33% for at least 30 days. By 60 days, only 18% of these detained offenders remained in placement; and by 90 days, less than 12% remained.

THE LEGAL RIGHTS OF JUVENILES AT DETENTION HEARINGS

States routinely give juveniles certain rights in detention hearings. Juveniles are generally given a notice of the charges for which they were taken into custody, adviced of their right to remain silent, informed of the right to have their parents present or have a reasonable opportunity to contact and consult with them, and are given a statement of the reason for continued detention (if that has been ordered). Furthermore, states also usually provide juveniles the right to an attorney.

FOR FURTHER CONSIDERATION

Questions for discussion

1. Should juveniles be detained longer than 24 h? If so, under what circumstances?
2. What factors are perhaps most important in determining if a juvenile should be continued in detention?

Review for chapter eight

Important terms to know:

Initial hearing: In the juvenile court, the initial hearing is the juvenile's first appearance in court in most instances.

Juvenile detention centers: These are the equivalents of jail for adults; it's where juveniles are kept until their court hearing.

Study guide questions

Choose the right answers from the choices below.

1. At the initial hearing, the judge or referee will typically appoint counsel if
   a. The family seems needy
   b. The family asks for appointed counsel
   c. The family doesn't know where to find an attorney
   d. The family would rather not spend their own money
2. If the child denies the allegations in the petition, the next step is to
   a. Lock up the juvenile
   b. Schedule an adult court hearing
   c. Schedule an adjudication hearing
   d. Decide what punishment will make the juvenile accept responsibility
3. In the U.S. Supreme Court case of *Schall v. Martin* (1984), the court decided that young people
   a. Could be held in preventative detention
   b. Could not be held in preventative detention
   c. Should have committed murder before being detained in a detention facility
   d. Should have no rights while in detention

chapter nine

Adjudication hearings

Hearings following the initial hearing

After a child has had an *intake hearing*, the next step in the process is an *initial hearing*. However, as you learned in Chapter 8, if a youth is in custody, a hearing should have been held within 24 h of being detained. Often, these kinds of hearings are called *detention hearings* and may take place in the detention facility. They help to determine whether the young person will be detained or released into the custody of his or her parents or guardian.

Ordinarily, though, the initial hearing is a child's first appearance in court. At the initial hearing, the judge or referee will appoint counsel for the child if this is needed or requested, and will advise the child and his or her parents of the charges, and of their rights in a juvenile proceeding.

If the child admits the allegations of the delinquency petition at this initial hearing, the court could proceed immediately with a *dispositional hearing*, particularly if all the players in the courtroom drama agree. Most typically, the dispositional hearing is scheduled for a future date.

The adjudication hearing

If the child denies the charges in the petition, then either the case may proceed directly to an *adjudication hearing* (sometimes called a *fact-finding hearing*), or it, too, may be scheduled for a future date. This may be necessary to arrange for witnesses or for the gathering of evidence by the attorney representing the child or the prosecuting attorney.

An adjudication hearing or fact-finding hearing, is a trial to determine the facts. That is, to discover if the facts support a finding that the juvenile committed the offense. The adjudication hearing is much like a trial in a criminal court. The greatest difference is that there is usually no jury in a juvenile court adjudication hearing. Usually, there is no jury and the judge or the referee sits as the fact-finder and renders a judgment. A prosecuting attorney presents the facts supporting the petition, and attempts to prove the allegations in the petition beyond a reasonable doubt. If the child is represented by counsel, the defense attorney has the right (just as the prosecutor does) to call witnesses, cross-examine those witnesses, and otherwise attempt to show there is

reasonable doubt as to the allegations. The juvenile has the right to testify on his or her own behalf, but cannot be compelled to testify against himself or herself.

If the judge or referee finds that the allegations have not been proved, the juvenile is dismissed from the juvenile court. If, on the other hand, the court finds that the facts have been proved, a judgment is entered finding that the juvenile is a delinquent and a dispositional hearing is scheduled.

If the prosecutor feels that the juvenile belongs in the adult rather than the juvenile court system, a waiver petition is filed. When this happens, the judge or referee must first determine if there is probable cause that the youth committed the offense. After that finding, the hearing officer decides whether the case should be waived to an adult court. The decision of the judge or referee may often hinge on whether the juvenile is amenable to treatment in the juvenile justice system. In his or her argument, the prosecutor may present the previous record of the juvenile, the seriousness of the offense, and point out that previous efforts at treatment were unsuccessful (Vito and Simonsen, 2004). If the waiver is approved, the juvenile is immediately transferred to the adult justice system. If the waiver is not approved, the case remains in juvenile court, and the case continues with adjudication or disposition.

It is up to the judge or referee in each case to make a decision about whether the juvenile is a delinquent under the juvenile court statutes of the particular state.

In this chapter, we present five different cases of young people who were referred to the court on petitions.

The options available to the judge or referee in an adjudication hearing

In an adjudication hearing, the judge or the referee has these options:

- Dismiss the petition and send the child home.
- Declare the child a delinquent and schedule a dispositional hearing.
- Waive the juvenile to the adult criminal system (if the prosecutor has requested a waiver).
- Carry the hearing over to a future date or adjourn for more evidence gathering before continuing.

AN IMPORTANT U.S. SUPREME COURT DECISION

In re Gault 387 U.S. 1, 87 S.Ct. 1428 (1967)

Gerald Gault, age 15, was on probation in Arizona for a minor property offense when, in 1964, he and a friend made a crank telephone call to an adult neighbor, asking her, "Are your cherries ripe today?" and "Do you have big bombers?" Identified by the neighbor, the youth were arrested and detained.

The victim did not appear at the adjudication hearing, and the court never resolved the issue of whether Gault made the "obscene" remarks. Gault was committed to a training school until age 21. The maximum sentence for an adult would have been a $50 fine or 2 months in jail.

An attorney obtained for Gault, after the trial, filed a writ of *habeas corpus* that was eventually heard by the U.S. Supreme Court. The issue presented in the case was that Gault's constitutional rights (to notice of charges, counsel, questioning of witnesses, protection against self-incrimination, a transcript of the proceedings, and appellate review) were denied.

The Supreme Court ruled that in hearings that could result in commitment to an institution, juveniles have the right to notice and counsel, to question witnesses, and to protection against self-incrimination. The Supreme Court did not rule on a juvenile's right to appellate review or transcripts, but encouraged the states to provide those rights.

The Supreme Court based its ruling on the fact that Gault was being punished rather than helped by the juvenile court. The Supreme Court explicitly rejected the doctrine of *parens patriae* as the founding principle of juvenile justice, describing the concept as murky and of dubious historical relevance. The Supreme Court concluded that the handling of Gault's case violated the due process clause of the 14th Amendment: "Juvenile court history has again demonstrated that unbridled discretion, however benevolently motivated, is frequently a poor substitute for principle and procedure."

You make the call in these adjudication hearing cases

You now know that an adjudication hearing is like a trial in adult court. In an adjudication hearing, the juvenile court judge or referee will hear the case and decide whether the juvenile should be adjudged a delinquent. It is up to you—as the judge or referee in each case—to determine if the individual child should be released or whether they should be declared a delinquent under the juvenile code of the state and proceed to a disposition hearing. Decide how you would handle these cases if you were the juvenile court hearing officer. Consider the facts in each case and decide what you would do. Write your decision in the space following each case. Be prepared to state your rationale for your decision and be ready to defend your decision.

The case of Ethan, age 15

Ethan is 15 years old and in the 10th grade. He is appearing in court on a petition that alleges home incorrigibility and home truancy. This is his first time before the court and the first time he has been detained in a juvenile facility. Since the allegations have to do with status offenses, he has been in a detention center with other nonviolent juvenile offenders.

Ethan lives with some unfortunate circumstances. His parents had a bad marriage that featured conflict and physical violence. He witnessed his mother stab his father and he was involved in the court proceedings that followed that assault. Subsequently, his mother went to prison, where she remains at this time. His father is very ill with kidney disease and receives weekly dialysis treatments. Ethan has more responsibility than the average teen his age; however, at the same time, Ethan has not followed rules set by his father. For instance, he has run away on three occasions.

Nonetheless, despite his behavior and the circumstances of his family life, he appears to be a bright young man with considerable potential. He has supportive adults in his life among his extended family and at his school. He attends a school designed to help students who struggle in larger high school settings. Ethan admits that he has not put forth his best effort in school or at home. He also admits that he has been smoking marijuana several times a week.

Ethan states that the period of detention has helped him understand the importance of following rules and he insists that he will do better.

YOU MAKE THE CALL

You make the call. As the hearing officer, what would you decide to do with Ethan? Should he be adjudicated a delinquent? Is it important that the juvenile court be involved in helping him straighten out his life? Write your decision and the reasons for your decision in the space below.

_____

_____

_____

_____

_____

_____

After you have made the call, feel free to go to the appendix and review the decision of the actual court hearing officer in this case. Compare your decision with his and review the rationale for the referee's decision. Then check out the follow-up. What happened to Ethan in the year following this hearing?

_____

_____

_____

JUVENILE JUSTICE DEFINITION

A status offense involves conduct that would not be a crime if it was committed by an adult. That is, status offenses are actions considered to be a violation of the law only because of the youth's status as a minor (typically anyone under 17 or 18 years of age). Common examples of status offenses include underage drinking, skipping school, and violating a local curfew law.

JUVENILE JUSTICE FACT

Until the mid 1970s, it was common for the juvenile delinquency system to handle status offense cases. Therefore, children who came to the court on petitions related to status offenses were subject to all dispositional or probationary options applied to delinquent youth, including incarceration. But, in 1974, Congress encouraged states to decriminalize status offenses by enacting the Juvenile Justice and Delinquency Prevention Act (JJDPA), which, among other things, established the Deinstitutionalization of Status Offenders (DSO) core requirement. In keeping with the DSO core requirement, states receiving federal grants under the JJDPA agreed to prohibit the locked placement of youth charged with status offenses, and reform their systems so that youth at risk for, or charged with, status offenses, and their families, would receive family-based and community-based services. In the early years of the JJDPA, between 1974 and 1980, the number of court referrals for status offenses decreased 21% and status offender detentions decreased 50%.

The case of Johnetta, age 16

Johnetta is 16 years old and is charged with one count of malicious destruction of property (over $1000), a second count of retail fraud, 3rd degree, and a third count of trespassing. She was involved with the juvenile court two years ago. At that time, she failed her initial term of probation and was then placed in a six-month residential treatment program. After successfully completing the program, she was released from the court's jurisdiction. Since that time, Johnetta has discontinued seeing her psychologist, stopped taking her medication, been suspended from school for 10 days, and begun smoking marijuana.

The malicious destruction of property charge results from accusations that she broke windows and a door after she was apprehended by a security guard at a discount department store for allegedly stealing clothes. She had not left the store when she was detained by the security staff, but became so irate she began running through the store and, when cornered and placed in a store office, began screaming, swearing, and throwing objects. She had been previously banned from this store for suspected shoplifting, which is why she is also charged with trespassing.

The prosecuting attorney plans to call the security guard and other store personnel to testify against Johnetta. Johnetta has already said that she didn't do anything wrong and is being picked on. She says she was at home alone when the incident occurred at the store.

YOU MAKE THE CALL

What would you decide? As the hearing officer, what would you decide to do with Johnetta? Should she be adjudicated a delinquent? Is it important that the juvenile court take jurisdiction over her? Write your decision and the reasons for your decision in the space below.

_____
_____
_____
_____
_____
_____
_____

After you have made the call, feel free to go to the appendix and review the decision of the actual court hearing officer in this case. Compare your decision with his, and review the rationale for the referee's decision. Then check out the follow-up. What happened to Johnetta in the year following this hearing?

_____
_____
_____

The case of Jacob, age 14

Jacob is 14 years old and is before the court on a petition for home incorrigibility and one count of domestic violence, in which his sister is the victim. He has been accused of failing to obey the rules at home, smoking marijuana excessively for at least the past year and a half, stealing money from family members, and was suspected of stealing $650 from the school art teacher two months before this hearing. The domestic violence charge is related to a fight he had with his sister, age 18, attacking her with a baseball bat. She sustained a broken arm and several bruises.

His mother, who is divorced from Jacob's father, has tried to coordinate services for Jacob. She has taken him to a psychiatric clinic, appealed to the rabbi at the synagogue his mother attends for counseling, and used all of the discipline skills she could muster. However, the police have been called to the home at least four times over the past year when Jacob was angry and out of control. The police took him to a local psychiatric hospital for children and adolescents, where he stayed for 72 h before being released. That led to him being referred to an outpatient psychiatric clinic, where he attended therapy sessions over two months before he refused to return. For every type of service his mother has attempted, Jacob's commitment and follow-through has been consistently poor.

YOU MAKE THE CALL

What would you do? As the judge or referee, what would you decide to do with Jacob? Write your decision in the space below.

_____
_____
_____
_____
_____
_____

After you have made the call, feel free to go to the appendix and review the decision of the actual intake referee in this case. Compare your decision with his, review the rationale for the referee's decision. Then check out the follow-up. What happened to Jacob in the year following this adjudication hearing?

_____
_____
_____

The case of Shayna, age 16

Shayna, 16 years old, is in the 10th grade at a charter school. She is appearing before the court on charges of larceny involving a weapon, retail fraud, 2nd degree, and stealing a financial transaction device. All three crimes occurred on the same day, while shopping at a mall with a friend. The two girls stole clothing items from Target, stole another shopper's purse (with a handgun inside) while she was trying on shoes, and a short time later, used her credit card to purchase a movie ticket and snacks. Shayna told the court worker that her friend was more experienced and influenced her in their bad decision making. Shayna did admit that she carried stolen items out of the Target store and also admitted knowing about the gun and credit card purchase.

Shayna has had no prior involvement with the police or the juvenile court. Both she and her parents say that she has never been in trouble before. She is an average student, and has had only occasional minor school problems previously. She has played on the basketball team at her school and been a cheerleader. She states that she plans to pursue a career in nursing.

She moved from another city in the county less than a year ago. Since moving, she has struggled to make new friends, admits trying marijuana, and is now four months pregnant. Because she attends a new school, she is not as invested with the teachers or other students as she was at her previous school. She says that her closest friend is her boyfriend, who resides next door.

YOU MAKE THE CALL

What would you do? As the judge or referee, what would you decide to do with Shayna? Write your decision in the space below.

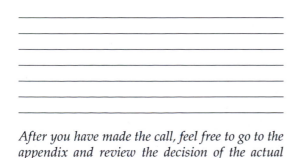

After you have made the call, feel free to go to the appendix and review the decision of the actual intake referee in this case. Compare your decision with his, review the rationale for the referee's decision. Then check out the follow-up. What happened to Shayna in the year following this adjudication hearing?

The case of Austin, age 17

Austin is 17 years old, but the offense currently before the court (possession of cocaine) occurred three days prior to his 17th birthday. Austin, however, has a long history of delinquency and it is likely that he is being formally charged with just a fraction of his actual offenses.

Austin has previously been adjudicated a delinquent, beginning at age 14. In the past, he was charged with selling and possessing drugs, robbery, assault, and drug use. He has been on probation and has received extensive services within the community through the juvenile drug court program. These services included inpatient substance abuse treatment, counseling, referral to Narcotics Anonymous, and psychiatric treatment.

Despite his near 18-month-long prior court involvement and his apparent success in the juvenile drug court program, Austin is returning to court on a new petition. He openly admits that he began smoking marijuana daily within two weeks of his dismissal from the court the last time. Additionally, he is pending a preliminary exam in an adult court in another county for a retail fraud, a robbery, a breaking and entering, and a financial fraud.

Additional information that comes to light at this hearing is that Austin is working as a parking attendant late at night, that his friend's home was raided recently by the police and drugs were confiscated, and that Austin's family has allowed another friend who is on probation to move into their home.

On the bright side, Austin appears to be doing well in school and is liked by the school staff. He is a senior and should be eligible to graduate in about a year if he continues to attend his high school.

YOU MAKE THE CALL

As the judge or referee, what would you decide to do with Austin? Write your decision in the space below.

_____
_____
_____
_____
_____
_____
_____

After you have made the call, review the decision of the actual judge or referee in this case. Compare your decision with his, review the rationale for the referee's decision. Then check out the follow-up. What happened to Austin in the year following this adjudication hearing?

_____
_____
_____

JUVENILE JUSTICE FACT

Even before the establishment of the first juvenile court in Illinois in 1899, there were laws and ordinances in some cities and states that allowed for courts to take jurisdiction over incorrigible youth. That is still a possibility today. But there are basically three parts to the definition of incorrigibility. To be "incorrigible," a child's actions must occur repeatedly and be disruptive, dangerous, disobedient, and in direct violation of lawful commands. One or two instances of disobedience could just be a part of growing up or being a teenager. Repeated, regularly occurring acts of disobedience may constitute a real problem.

Furthermore, the child's actions must also threaten the welfare, order, and/or safety of the environment and those near the child. Disorderly conduct in school, as well as drug or alcohol use, would fall into this category.

Finally, the orders that the child is violating must be legal commands. A child cannot be found incorrigible for disobeying illegal orders such as those that force the child to commit a crime or submit to being abused or hurt. Commands that violate the child's rights, such as his or her religious freedom, are also unlawful.

A U.S. SUPREME COURT DECISION YOU SHOULD KNOW

McKeiver v. Pennsylvania 403 U.S. 528, 91 S.Ct. 1976 (1971)

Joseph McKeiver, age 16, was charged with robbery, larceny, and receiving stolen goods. He and 20 to 30 other youths allegedly chased three youths and took 25 cents from them. McKeiver met with his attorney for only a few minutes before his adjudicatory hearing. At the hearing, his attorney's request for a jury trial was denied by the court. He was subsequently adjudicated and placed on probation.

The State Supreme Court cited recent decisions of the U.S. Supreme Court that had attempted to include more due process in juvenile court proceedings without eroding the essential benefits of the juvenile court. The State Supreme Court affirmed the lower court, arguing that of all due process rights, trial by jury is most likely to "destroy the traditional character of juvenile proceedings."

The U.S. Supreme Court found that the due process clause of the 14th Amendment did not require jury trials in juvenile court. The impact of the U.S. Supreme Court's *Gault* and *Winship* decisions was to enhance the accuracy of the juvenile court process at the fact-finding stage. In *McKeiver*, the U.S. Supreme Court argued that juries are not known to be more accurate than judges in the adjudication stage and could be disruptive to the informal atmosphere of the juvenile court, tending to make it more adversarial.

FOR FURTHER CONSIDERATION

Questions for discussion

1. Should juveniles be represented by attorneys in adjudication hearings? Why or why not?
2. What might be some of the implications of a judge or referee declaring a youth a juvenile delinquent?

Review for chapter nine

Important terms to know:

Adjudication Hearing: A hearing to determine the facts in a juvenile court hearing. The adjudication hearing is much like a trial in a criminal court.

Incorrigibility: To be incorrigible, a child's actions must occur repeatedly and be disruptive, dangerous, disobedient, and in direct violation of lawful commands. Many state juvenile codes still allow juveniles to be charged with being incorrigible.

Study guide questions

Choose the right answers from the choices below.

1. In an adjudication hearing, the judge or the referee has several options, including
   a. Dismissing the petition against the minor
   b. Finding the juvenile to be a nuisance
   c. Sentencing the child to prison
   d. Imposing the death penalty
2. In the landmark juvenile justice case *In re Gault* (1967), the U.S. Supreme Court based its ruling on the opinion that
   a. Gault was a minor
   b. Gault was obscene
   c. Gault lied in court
   d. Gault was being punished rather than helped
3. The U.S. Supreme Court in the *In re Gault* decision explicitly rejected the doctrine of *parens patriae* as the founding principle of juvenile justice, describing the concept as
   a. Too old to be useful
   b. Murky and of dubious historical relevance
   c. Unhelpful because we no longer have kings
   d. Parents are old fashioned
4. In 1974, Congress encouraged states to decriminalize status offenses by enacting the Juvenile Justice and Delinquency Prevention Act (JJDPA), which
   a. Said it was okay to lock up kids with adults
   b. Rejected the idea of detention for juveniles
   c. Established the deinstitutionalization of status offenders
   d. Declared status offenses as unconstitutional
5. The U.S. Supreme Court found in *McKeiver v. Pennsylvania* (1971) that the due process clause of the 14th Amendment
   a. Did not allow jury trials for juveniles
   b. Required that juveniles have jury trials in every adjudication hearing
   c. Suggested that jury trials were fairer than judges
   d. Did not require jury trials in juvenile courts

chapter ten

Disposition hearings

The disposition hearing

As you learned in the previous chapter, if the child denies the charges in the petition, then either the case may proceed directly to an adjudication hearing or it may be scheduled for a future date. This may be necessary to arrange for witnesses or for the gathering of evidence by the attorney representing the child or by the prosecuting attorney.

And, further, you learned that the adjudication hearing is a trial to determine the facts. Usually, there is no jury, and the judge or the referee sits as the fact-finder and renders a judgment. If the judge or referee finds that the allegations have not been proved, the juvenile is dismissed from the juvenile court. If, on the other hand, the court finds that the facts have been proved, a judgment is entered (finding that the juvenile is a delinquent) and a dispositional hearing is scheduled.

If the child admits the allegations of the delinquency petition at any stage—for instance, at an initial hearing or in an adjudication hearing—or, if the young person is adjudged a delinquent and the facts alleged in the petition are found to be true, then the court proceeds to schedule a dispositional hearing, particularly if the child, his or her parents, and the prosecuting attorney (representing the state) agrees. Most typically, the dispositional hearing is scheduled for a future date.

A juvenile court disposition hearing is basically the sentencing portion of a juvenile trial. The purpose of such a hearing is to determine the most appropriate form of treatment or custody for the juvenile offender.

In this regard, juvenile proceedings are distinct from adult criminal trials. Adult criminal court sentences tend to be oriented toward sanctions and punishments. Sentencing in a juvenile court tends to focus more on rehabilitating the minor rather than punishing him or her for a wrongdoing. That is why, in the disposition hearing, the court referee or judge attempts to provide the juvenile with treatment, rehabilitation, or training, as an alternative to incarceration.

Bifurcated courts

Most juvenile courts today are bifurcated. This means that the adjudication hearing and the disposition hearing are held separately (Taylor and Fritsch, 2011). One significant reason as to why they are held as two separate

hearings may be related to what is allowed in each hearing. Adjudication hearings are formal court hearings that follow typical court procedures in terms of the evidence presented. Disposition hearings are less formal, and strict rules of evidence usually don't apply. That is, testimony presented can be hearsay evidence and opinions. However, many states grant the juvenile the right to counsel during a disposition hearing, and also, maybe, the right to confront and cross-examine witnesses.

Often, the probation officer who submitted the original social history report or the predisposition report, will present evidence based on that predisposition report. The defense attorney and the prosecutor are afforded the opportunity to challenge information contained in the predisposition report.

Similarly, if a psychological or psychiatric evaluation was conducted, the mental health examiner may be called as an expert witness to present testimony regarding a disposition. Both the defense attorney and the prosecutor would have the opportunity to cross-examine that witness.

What is determined during a disposition hearing?

During a disposition hearing, the juvenile court judge or referee will focus on three key questions to help determine what the consequences of the offense will be. These three questions will be part of the judge or referee's thinking:

- Is the child in serious need of rehabilitation or counseling?
- Is protection needed for the child or for the general public?
- Should the child be placed on probation?

The answers to these three key questions will, of course, vary, depending on each individual minor's case. But there are some other factors that the judge or referee will analyze during the disposition hearing:

- The juvenile laws of that particular jurisdiction or state.
- The nature and seriousness of the crime committed by the juvenile defendant.

- The child's history of previous offenses and crimes.
- The local juvenile court's polices and the community's social standards regarding juvenile sentencing practices.
- The available resources to help bring about rehabilitation for the minor.

At the completion of the disposition hearing, the judge or referee will decide on the appropriate disposition of the case.

In this chapter, we present three different cases of young people who have been declared delinquent, but are awaiting disposition hearings to determine what will happen to them. Acting as the judge or referee, you have a chance in each case to make decisions about what happens to the juvenile as a result of their offense.

The options available to the judge or referee in a disposition hearing

As you might expect at this point, the judge or referee may have an unlimited number of options in terms of rehabilitation and protection of both the child and the community. However, the unlimited number of options will be tempered by the resources available within the county or the state. Keep in mind that "available resources" refer not only to the programs or facilities that are options for the court, but also to the budget granted to the juvenile court by the county for treatment and rehabilitation services. In general, though, these are some of the options available for the court in deciding a child's disposition:

- Suspension of judgment: The judge or referee does not give a specific disposition. Instead, he or she can postpone the disposition of the juvenile if the child agrees to abide by certain conditions. If the juvenile abides by these conditions within a certain period of time, the judge or referee does not impose the sentence. If the juvenile fails to abide by the conditions, then the disposition is imposed.
  - Probation
  - Detention in a juvenile facility
  - Placement in a county or state residential facility
  - Individual or family therapy
  - Intensive probation
  - House arrest
  - Electronic monitoring or tethering
  - Boot camp
  - Community service
  - Psychological evaluation
  - Referral to a psychiatrist for possible medication
  - Fine or reimbursement to the victim

- Anger management class
- Parent training classes for parents
- Placement with a relative or in a foster home

LEARNING MORE

In coming up with a disposition, the juvenile court has two main goals: (1) to serve the best interests of the delinquent minor by providing care, treatment, and guidance to rehabilitate the child, and enable him or her to be a law-abiding and productive member of his or her family, and the community, in the future and (2) to provide for the protection and safety of the public.

To best reach these goals, juvenile courts are authorized to order delinquent wards to receive care, treatment, and guidance that is consistent with their best interests, that hold them accountable for their behavior, and that is appropriate for their circumstances. This guidance may include punishment that is consistent with the rehabilitative objectives of juvenile court laws. It may also include detention in a secure residential facility or a long-term treatment program. However, courts have to always be mindful of placing youth first in the least restrictive environment.

Juvenile court judges and referees have broad discretion during dispositions to try to reach juvenile justice goals. Usually, the dispositional orders of a judge or referee will only be reversed by a higher court if it can be shown that there was an abuse of discretion.

You make the call in these disposition hearing cases

You have learned that a disposition hearing is a hearing in which a plan is made for the juvenile to help bring about treatment and rehabilitation. This hearing takes place after the adjudication hearing in which a finding was made that the child is a delinquent. It is now up to you—as the judge or referee in each case—to determine what kind of plan should be put in place to best help this young person to make a positive adjustment.

Should the minor be placed on probation? Should he or she be ordered into psychological treatment? Or should the order specify that the youth be confined to a residential treatment facility? Decide what you think is best for each juvenile in this chapter after reading about their offense and their background. Write your decision in the space following each case. Be prepared to state your rationale for your decision and be ready to defend your decision.

The case of Jamal, age 16

Jamal is 16 years old and lives with his father and stepmother. He is before the court for disposition on counts of home truancy and home incorrigibility. Jamal reports that he has been physically and emotionally abused by his father and refuses to return home. Child Protective Service (CPS) has been to the home and conducted an investigation; however, CPS has been unable to substantiate Jamal's allegations. His father denies them as well. Regardless, if Jamal is returned home, his safety is at risk, as there is a strong possibility he will continue to truant. Additionally, Jamal has a history of depression and has threatened to kill himself. Returning him home may intensify these feelings.

Jamal's father wants his son at home, and he is not supportive of any other plan. However, the father's actions are of concern. For instance, he has not visited with Jamal while he has been in a county residential facility awaiting his disposition, nor has he called to check on him. Even after the referee spoke with the father about the importance of visiting, he still did not visit. The father said he tried to visit his son, but was turned away. If this is true, it is true that he did not try to visit on any other occasion. Furthermore, he failed to show up at the court caseworker's office for two social history meetings, and, when pressured to meet briefly after the initial hearing, he appeared disinterested and eager to leave.

A short-term probationary plan with Jamal's paternal great-aunt was considered, but a primary component of that plan was counseling and neither she nor Jamal's father ever called the court worker to indicate that they had tried to arrange counseling—as they were advised to do. In addition, regarding the idea of Jamal living with the great-aunt, both the great-aunt and the father agreed it could be for only one month. It appeared to the court worker that even with intensive counseling, very little progress could be made in that short time period so that Jamal could successfully return home. Given the family's lack of follow-through, this plan does not appear supportive enough for Jamal's and his father's needs.

The court caseworker recommended that Jamal participate in a residential treatment program, as it appeared to be the best solution at the time. That is the plan that Jamal liked best, and the court worker reasoned that during the time in a residential treatment program, he would be safe, he likely would not truant, and he could—it was hoped—focus on his own goals. While in a residential treatment facility, Jamal and his father would be able to participate in counseling in the program on a consistent basis for a significant length of time. It is hoped that they can repair their relationship enough during this time so that Jamal will want to return home.

The court caseworker learned that Jamal's mother made plans to return to the area in the near future. If she does move back into the same city, as she has promised, this will allow her the opportunity to support Jamal, participate in counseling at the treatment facility, and discuss custody arrangements with Jamal's father.

It is important to note, too, that since Jamal has been detained, he has not been attending his high school, therefore, he has fallen behind. His education and current standing in school must be considered in any plan.

YOU MAKE THE CALL

Now you make the call. As the hearing officer, what would you decide to do with Jamal? Should he be released to live with his great-aunt? Or should he be sent to a treatment facility for juveniles? In either case, how long should the next plan be? How can his mother be best involved in his future? Write your decision in the space below.

_____
_____
_____
_____
_____
_____
_____

After you have made the call, feel free to go to the appendix and review the decision of the actual court hearing officer in this case. Compare your decision with hers and review the rationale for the judge or referee's decision. Then check out the follow-up. What happened to Jamal in the year following his disposition hearing?

_____

_____

_____

JUVENILE JUSTICE FACT

The majority of youths processed through the juvenile courts in this country are adjudicated delinquent, regardless of the offense. And of those youngsters who are adjudicated, about 57% are placed on probation.

About 86,000 young people under the age of 21 are detained or confined in public and private detention centers, group homes, camps, ranches, and other correctional institutions. The average cost per day is $240.99 for each individual youth placed in a state-funded residential facility.

The case of Melissa, age 14

Melissa is 14 years old and is the oldest of two children in her family. Melissa was referred to the juvenile court for truancy from school, however, this was a problem that started about three years ago when the family lived in another city.

Melissa lives with both parents; however, her parents are divorced. Melissa and her 12-year-old brother were living with their mother after the divorce, which occurred two years ago, but their mother was having financial problems and they moved in with their father. This "father" is not the biological father of Melissa and her brother. The mother gave birth to her two children before she was married and their biological father has not been involved in their life and neither Melissa nor her brother know who he is. Melissa's mother met the man they consider to be their father in a bar.

The divorce occurred two years ago after their father had been charged with domestic violence against their mother. The mother says that Melissa and her brother Bryan were never abused by him. However, both Bryan and Melissa have witnessed their mother being abused and both have tried to break it up when they were fighting or arguing.

Melissa's mother reports that Melissa started missing school in the last couple of years because of the influence of their father, who wasn't strict with Melissa about attending school. A year ago, the school referred Melissa to a counseling program and while she was seeing a caseworker for counseling her school attendance improved.

When her mother talks about Melissa's developmental history, she says she (mother) was depressed and that she cannot recall much about Melissa's infancy. She did describe Melissa as a quiet and contented child. She adjusted well to kindergarten and did well academically with all As through the sixth grade. By the sixth grade she began to develop problems, including conflicts with other girls and with at least one teacher.

It was during the sixth grade that marriage problems for the parents became worse. By the seventh grade, the mother and children moved to a different city, but school truancy problems developed for Melissa. Melissa told the court caseworker that she did not like school and that's why she didn't go. "I'm good at it," she said, "but it's a waste of time." She said she got into the habit in the seventh grade of not going to school, and it had become increasingly difficult to go regularly.

Melissa says she has a poor relationship with her father, but she is close to her mother (even though they have fought over going to school) and her brother. She said she started drinking alcohol at age 12, drinking daily for several weeks or months. By age 14, she was drinking less, but started using marijuana frequently. She says that she has stopped using marijuana.

The court caseworker referred Melissa for a psychological evaluation. The results show that she scored a verbal scale IQ of 94 (average), a performance scale IQ of 98 (average), and a full scale IQ of 95 (average). Her achievement grades show a high school reading level, but she does arithmetic at only the eighth grade level. Personality testing indicated that she is a self-centered girl who tends to lack insight. She tends to be defiant and oppositional. She appears to be rather manipulative and to see the world in terms of power and control. The psychologist recommended intensive probation, an anger management group, and referral of her parents to parent training, as well as referral of mother to a domestic violence shelter.

The intake referee was at first considering the consent docket, however, she thought that the court should be more directly involved in order to help make sure Melissa goes to school and that the family issues get addressed. Melissa was sent to court for an adjudication hearing and was made a delinquent. The next step is a disposition hearing.

YOU MAKE THE CALL

As the judge in this case, what would you decide to do with Melissa? Write your decisions for her disposition in the space below.

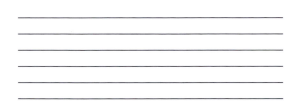

After you have made the call, feel free to go to the appendix and review the decision of the actual judge in this case. Compare your decision with his and review the rationale for the judge's decision. Then check out the follow-up. What happened to Melissa in the year following this disposition hearing?

_____

_____

_____

Learning more about dispositions

A number of states have created "blended" sentencing structures for cases involving serious and repeat juvenile offenders, as a mechanism for holding these youth accountable for their offenses, while retaining the court's ability to provide the most effective options. According to its report on state responses to violent youth crime, the National Center for Juvenile Justice has defined these blended sentencing measures as "the imposition of juvenile and/or adult correctional sanctions to cases involving serious and violent juvenile offenders who have been adjudicated in juvenile court or convicted in criminal court."

In other words, this expanded sentencing authority may allow criminal and juvenile courts to impose either juvenile or adult sentences, or both, in cases involving juveniles. However, such procedures are simply mechanisms for taking "hard cases" out of the juvenile justice system. While such policies and procedures have been available for as long as there have been juvenile courts, in recent years these mechanisms have become a much more prominent feature of the states' approaches to serious juvenile offending.

Transfer laws—which spell out conditions under which juveniles may be prosecuted in the same manner as adults—have tended to increase, to become more expansive in their scope, and more automatic in their operation. And *blended sentencing* laws—which can expose even those who remain under juvenile court jurisdiction to the risk of adult criminal sanctions—have become commonplace as well.

One type of blended sentence allows juvenile courts to impose juvenile as well as adult sanctions or dispositions simultaneously, while suspending the adult sanction. If the youth follows the conditions of the juvenile sentence, and commits no further violation, the adult sentence is revoked. This type of sentencing authority has become popular in such states as Connecticut, Kentucky, and Minnesota. If the youth is involved in further trouble, the adult sanction can be imposed.

IMPORTANT INFORMATION ABOUT THE DETENTION OF YOUTH

One in five youths is detained between the time of referral or petition to the juvenile court and the time the case disposition happens (Snyder and Sickmund, 2006). The Uniform Juvenile Court Act, first passed by Congress in 1968, says this about detention:

> A child taken into custody may not be detained or placed in shelter care prior to the hearing on the petition unless the child's detention or care is required to protect the person or property of others or of the child or because the child may abscond or be removed from the jurisdiction of the court or because the child has no parent, guardian, or custodian or other person able to provide supervision and care for the child and return the child to the court when required, or an order for the child's detention or shelter care has been made by the court pursuant to this chapter (Hess, 2010, p. 272).

The intent of this Act and the intent of subsequent policies coming from such organizations as the National Juvenile Detention Association are to protect children from the harm of exposing them to criminals and from the degrading effects of jails, lockups, and holding cells (Hess, 2010).

Juvenile justice experts have stressed that detention is a process, not a place, and that those in charge of secure detention facilities understand how detention practices should be related to larger juvenile justice goals (Griffin and Torbet, 2002). In addition, detention options should be short-term, designed to safeguard the community, and to offer rehabilitation (Hess, 2010).

COALITION FOR JUVENILE JUSTICE

In 2001, the Coalition for Juvenile Justice (CJJ), a nationwide coalition of the state advisory groups and allies dedicated to preventing children and youth from becoming involved in the courts, and upholding the highest standards of care when youth are charged with wrongdoing and enter the justice system, began a multiyear partnership with Annie E. Casey Foundation of Baltimore, Maryland, to promote and develop detention reform throughout the United States. In 2003, CJJ published a major report, *Unlocking the Future: Detention Reform in the Juvenile Justice System*, which provides evidence to show that, contrary to popular belief, the majority of detained youth are not the older, violent offenders that the public assumes need to be under lock and key.

Citing compelling evidence, the report demonstrated that juvenile court jurisdictions throughout the United States needlessly place young people with mental health, substance abuse, and family problems—most of whom are 15 years or younger, nonviolent, and disproportionately youth of color—into locked detention.

The CJJ continues to work with the Casey Foundation to advance the Foundation's long-range project, the Juvenile Detention Alternatives Initiative, which includes, as major objectives: (1) reducing the number of children inappropriately detained and (2) improving public safety and conditions of juvenile confinement.

The Coalition for Juvenile Justice website is at http://www.juvjustice.org/.

FOR FURTHER CONSIDERATION

Questions for discussion

1. If a judge or referee opts to send a juvenile to a residential facility, how can you tell if it is punishment or treatment?
2. Should only older and violent juveniles be confined in residential facilities?

Review for chapter ten

Important terms to know:

Disposition hearing: The disposition hearing in a juvenile court is like the sentencing portion of an adult trial. The purpose of such a hearing is to determine the most appropriate form of treatment or custody for juvenile offenders.

Predisposition report: A report prepared by the juvenile court staff, often the probation officer, who submits this report to the judge or referee to help with decision making. The report may be called the social history report in some jurisdictions.

Suspension of judgment: Suspension of judgment means that the judge or referee does not give a specific disposition. Instead, he or she can postpone the disposition for the juvenile if the juvenile agrees to abide by certain conditions.

Intensive probation: A type of probation that involves more frequent contact between the intensive probation officer and the juvenile, and typically involves more treatment services.

House arrest: Sometimes house arrest is imposed as a condition of probation. It generally means that the juvenile is confined to his or her house for a period of time.

Tether: A tether is an electronic monitoring device, often attached to a juvenile (frequently to his or her ankle) that tracks his or her whereabouts, and issues a report to the probation officer or the court.

Community service: A type of disposition that involves some type of service or volunteer work in the community. For instance, it could mean the juvenile has to perform a certain number of hours in community services such as working in a library, or with a park clean-up crew, or in work for some other nonprofit agency.

Study guide questions

Choose the right answers from the choices below.

1. During a disposition hearing, the juvenile court judge or referee will focus on specific key questions to help determine what the consequences of the offense will be. These key questions would include
   a. How much money does the family earn?
   b. Is protection needed for the child or for the general public?
   c. Should the child be placed in 24-h restraints?
   d. How cruel should the punishment be?

2. The judge or referee may have an unlimited number of options in terms of rehabilitation and protection of both the child and the community; however, the unlimited number of options will be
   a. Tempered by the resources available within the county or the state.
   b. Dependent on the power and status of the parents.
   c. Tempered by the race of the juvenile.
   d. Dependent on the whims of the judge.
3. Of the juveniles adjudicated in juvenile courts in this country, about _____ are placed on probation.
   a. 25%
   b. 39%
   c. 57%
   d. 79%
4. A number of states have created "blended" sentencing structures for cases involving serious and repeat juvenile offenders. Blended sentencing involves
   a. The imposition of jail or prison terms.
   b. The imposition of juvenile and/or adult correctional sanctions, or both.
   c. The imposition of the death penalty.
   d. The imposition of weak or ineffective sanctions.
5. The Uniform Juvenile Court Act, first passed by Congress in 1968, says this about juvenile detention
   a. A juvenile cannot be detained prior to a hearing on the petition.
   b. A juvenile can be detained if he or she is at least 12 years old.
   c. A juvenile cannot be detained unless it is to teach him or her a lesson.
   d. A juvenile may not be detained prior to the hearing on the petition unless the child's detention or care is required to protect the person or property of others.

section four

Transferring juveniles to adult courts:
You make the call in waiver hearings

chapter eleven

Waiver hearings

Waiver hearings for juveniles

Some juvenile cases are transferred to adult courts in a procedure called a *waiver*. Typically, juvenile cases that are subjected to waiver involve serious offenses, like rape or murder, or juveniles who have been in trouble before. Minors cannot just be waived to an adult criminal court; they have a right to a hearing to determine if their case should be transferred to an adult court.

In most states, a juvenile offender must be at least 16 to be eligible for waiver to adult court. But, in a number of states, minors as young as 13 could be subjected to a waiver petition. And a few states allow children of *any* age to be tried as adults for certain types of crimes, such as homicide.

Factors that might lead a court to grant a waiver petition and transfer a juvenile case to adult court include

- The juvenile being charged with a particularly serious offense.
- The juvenile having a lengthy juvenile record.
- The minor being older than 16, usually.
- The failure of past efforts to rehabilitate the juvenile.
- The expectation that youth services would have to work with the juvenile for a long time in order for rehabilitation to take place.

There are three ways that transfer proceedings can begin. The first, and most common, is that the prosecutor requests a waiver. The second is that the juvenile court judge initiates transfer proceedings. And the third is that some state laws require that juveniles be tried as adults in certain types of serious, violent cases.

If the prosecutor or judge seeks to transfer the case to an adult court, the minor is entitled to a hearing and representation by an attorney. This hearing is called the *waiver hearing*, *fitness hearing*, or *certification hearing*. Usually, the prosecutor must show probable cause that the juvenile actually committed the offense listed in the petition.

If the prosecutor has established probable cause, the judge must then decide on the minor's chances at rehabilitation as a juvenile. To make this decision, the judge will often hear evidence on the minor's background, his or her juvenile court record, and his or her willingness to get treatment in the juvenile system.

If the judge transfers the juvenile to the adult criminal court, the case starts there at the beginning—typically, with the arraignment.

Some states have "automatic transfer" laws that require juvenile cases to be transferred to adult criminal court if the offender is a certain age or older (usually 16) and if the charges involve a serious or violent offense. Minors subjected to an automatic transfer can still request a transfer hearing in juvenile court. During that hearing—called a *reverse waiver* or *reverse transfer hearing*—the juvenile (through an attorney) has the burden of convincing the judge to reverse the automatic transfer and allow the juvenile to be tried in juvenile court.

The purpose of waiver to an adult court

Juveniles are waived to adult criminal courts for prosecution for three basic reasons:

- To remove juvenile offenders charged with heinous, violent offenses that frequently generate media and community pressure
- To remove chronic offenders who have exhausted the resources and the patience of the juvenile justice system
- To impose longer potential sentences than those available within the juvenile justice system (Taylor and Fritsch, 2011)

In regards to the third reason, some people argue that the primary reason for transferring a youth to an adult court is to make sure they get a more severe sentence than those allowed in the juvenile court. There are limited maximum terms available in the juvenile court. That is, each state sets what is known as a jurisdictional age limit, which specifies the age when a juvenile court no longer has jurisdiction over a juvenile offender. Depending on the state, the jurisdictional age limit is usually between ages 19 and 21. In eight states, including Alaska, Iowa, Kentucky, and Texas, the jurisdictional age limit is 19. In 31 states, including Alabama, Arizona, the District of Columbia, Massachusetts, Michigan, and New York, the age limit is 21. However, the age limit is 22 in Florida, 23 in Kansas, and 25 in California, Montana, Oregon, and Wisconsin (Taylor and Fritsch, 2011). What this means is that once a juvenile has reached the jurisdictional age limit, they must be released from the juvenile court and from the sanctions imposed on them.

In a waiver hearing, the judge or referee has only two options:

1. Waive the juvenile to adult court.
2. Reject the waiver request and retain the minor in the juvenile court system.

JUVENILE JUSTICE FACT

According to the Office of Juvenile Justice and Delinquency Prevention, the estimated number of cases transferred from a juvenile court to a criminal court for adults peaked in 1994 at 13,100 cases, more than double the number of cases waived in 1985. In 2010, juvenile courts waived an estimated 6,000 delinquency cases, 55% fewer cases than in 1994.

You make the call in these waiver hearing cases

The case of Joseph, age 16

Joseph is 16 years old, and has been involved with the juvenile court for three years. He was originally petitioned to the court on charges of theft, robbery, breaking and entering, and felonious assault. He has been on probation, participated in an outpatient program for teens on probation, and spent 12 months in a county juvenile treatment facility. He began receiving mental health treatment at the age of four and has participated in counseling services for most of his life. He went for several years to individual counseling sessions through a family service agency, and, more recently, received home-based therapy through a public counseling agency.

While in the county residential treatment program, he received quality, individualized therapy throughout his year-long stay. According to the therapist, he made good progress and was seemingly very prepared to return home. After successfully completing the residential program, several support systems were put into place to ensure a positive transition back into the community. For instance, his mother moved from the city where he got into his previous trouble to a suburban community, where he was introduced to the high school football coach. In addition, the juvenile court provided him with the equipment he needed, and arrangements were made for him to have transportation to and from practices. Also, home-based therapy was in place to begin as soon as he moved back home.

Joseph began playing on the school football team, but suddenly quit about a month after he returned home. His mother reported that he had a strong desire to be around his old friends and was continually drawn back to the city and those friends. Joseph openly admitted to his probation officer that he began drinking alcohol and smoking marijuana within weeks of leaving the county facility.

Joseph was apprehended by the police four months after he had been home, and was charged with the armed robbery of a liquor store. The petition stated that he used a gun in this robbery and that he was with three older teens, one of whom was driving a stolen car during the robbery. After review of the petition by the prosecutor's office, that office requested a waiver to have Joseph tried as an adult.

YOU MAKE THE CALL

As the hearing officer, what would you decide to do with Joseph? Should he be waived to an adult court for a trial? Or should he be retained in the juvenile court, with renewed efforts to help him with rehabilitation? Write your decision in the space below.

_____
_____
_____
_____
_____
_____

After you have made the call, feel free to go to the appendix and review the decision of the actual court hearing officer in this case. Compare your decision with his, and review the rationale for the judge's decision. Then check out the follow-up. What happened to Joseph in the year following this waiver hearing?

_____
_____
_____

LEARNING MORE

A major concern, when waiving or transferring a juvenile to an adult court, is about the juvenile's competence to stand trial. Is the juvenile competent? That is, does the juvenile have the ability to function effectively as a defendant in a criminal—or even, for that matter, in a juvenile—proceeding?

An individual is deemed competent when he or she can assist counsel in his or her defense, and is capable of effectively participating in the process and making decisions about his or her rights. This concern—and the questions raised—is much more complex than it may appear. The issue of competence goes well beyond a juvenile's IQ (intelligence quotient), academic achievement levels, or grades in school. Emerging brain research has revealed that the parts of the brain responsible for executive functions, such as the ability to assess risk and think about future consequences, to plan for the future, and delay impulses, are still developing well into the 20s for many individuals. But it is the brain's executive functions that figure the delinquency and criminal conducts so strongly.

In general, there has been little recognition in our society that young people, if they are sent to a criminal court, may well be incompetent to functionally assist in their trial because of developmental immaturity. It is one thing to hold juveniles accountable for their behavior; it is another thing to expect them to function at a level far beyond their capacity and competence.

The case of Jason, age 17

Jason is 17 years old and is appearing in the juvenile court for the first time. The charges he is facing are two counts of home invasion, 1st degree, one count of larceny of a firearm, one count of criminal sexual conduct, 2nd degree, and one count of retail fraud. All offenses occurred on two different days in the same week, but prior to his 17th birthday.

Jason has had an extremely traumatic childhood. He was born in a large city where he lived with his mother until he was almost four years old. He described his mother as a drug user, alcoholic, and a prostitute. There were always several men in their home and he suspects that one of them may be his father, but he is unsure. His mother frequently left him home alone and, on one occasion, while alone, their apartment caught fire. He was very frightened and didn't know what to do, so he hid underneath a bed. He passed out and was ultimately rescued by the city firefighters. As a result of this fire, he has major scars on his legs, arms, and stomach. Skin grafts were needed, but his mother declined and, instead, attempted to "scrub the scars away." He also now suffers from a severe case of asthma and is on several different inhalers. Jason wonders why his mother was not home at the time of the fire and sometimes suspects that she may have started the fire purposely.

Shortly after the fire, Jason's mother committed an assault with intent to commit murder and an armed robbery, and was sentenced to five to twenty years in prison. Jason was then placed in a guardianship with his grandparents; however, his grandfather died few months later. His grandmother raised him alone.

Jason participated in eight years of outpatient counseling and was hospitalized twice for inpatient services. He has been diagnosed with ADHD (attention deficit hyperactivity disorder), oppositional defiant disorder, and severe depression, and he has been prescribed several different medications.

Jason seems to be in great need of ongoing therapy and psychiatric services. He takes full responsibility for his offenses, but minimizes the seriousness. He appears to be a smart young man and is within three credits of earning his high-school diploma. He is not a drug user and is not involved with gangs. He recently began drinking alcohol, but described it as an attempt to deal with his depression.

Immediately after being arrested, Jason was lodged in the county jail where he remains, awaiting court proceedings. While there, it is reported that he has been respectful and cooperative. After review of the petition by the prosecutor's office, that office requested a waiver to have Jason tried as an adult.

YOU MAKE THE CALL

As the hearing officer, what would you decide to do with Jason? Should he be waived to an adult court for a trial? Or should he be retained in the juvenile court, with renewed efforts to help him with rehabilitation? Write your decision in the space below.

———————————————————
———————————————————
———————————————————
———————————————————
———————————————————
———————————————————

After you have made the call, feel free to go to the appendix and review the decision of the actual court hearing officer in this case. Compare your decision with his and review the rationale for the judge's decision. Then check out the follow-up. What happened to Jason in the year following this waiver hearing?

———————————————————
———————————————————
———————————————————

ONCE WAIVED, DO JUVENILES RECEIVE MORE SEVERE SENTENCES IN ADULT COURTS?

According to several studies, juveniles waived to an adult court are more likely to be sentenced to prison than any other potential disposition, such as probation (Taylor and Fritsch, 2011). Still, there is no guarantee that juveniles waived to adult courts will receive a lengthy prison sentence. One reason for this is that waived juveniles can be viewed as first-time offenders whose age tends to work in their favor, rather than lead to longer sentencing decisions. Juveniles waived to adult courts for the first time are generally given the same kinds of leniency accorded to first-time adult offenders (Taylor and Fritsch, 2011).

The case of Kimberly

Kimberly is 16 years old, but will turn 17 in two months. She is before the court for the first time for one count of armed robbery and one count of possession of a firearm during the commission of a felony.

At first, Kimberly failed to take responsibility for her crimes and minimized her offense. She said that she was shopping with her sister and two friends, one of whom brought along what she thought was a toy gun. While in her sister's car, leaving the store, they were all loudly singing a rap song with threatening lyrics that included phrases like "run your pockets." A woman was standing outside, near their car, smoking a cigarette. Kimberly said that this woman must have thought they were talking to her and felt threatened, and she called the police to report them. Kimberly and her friends, though, left the parking lot, drove to a liquor store for snacks, and when they came out of the store were arrested by the police.

Kimberly first stated that she never touched the gun or even looked at the victim. She added that the victim called the police "for no reason." She stated, "I didn't rob her, she was wrong." Later, in the conversation with a court worker, Kimberly tearfully admitted to holding the gun in her hand and waving it up and down in front of her to the beat of the music. She still denied knowledge that the gun was loaded, denied pointing it at the victim, and denied seeing that the woman had two young children with her. Ultimately, Kimberly admitted to loudly rapping the threatening words while waving a loaded gun and looking at the victim. She said she now felt remorseful and explained that this type of behavior was out of character for her.

Kimberly has a poor school history. She has two high school credits and a GPA of 0.5. She admits to skipping classes with her friends in the past and then missing a significant amount of school due to becoming pregnant and not having childcare. Kimberly's daughter is now two years old.

Kimberly associates with a group of friends who have been in trouble, have dropped out of school, and have minimal parental supervision. She and her sister both have children by brothers who are currently serving prison sentences.

After review of the petition by the prosecutor's office, that office requested a waiver to have Kimberly tried as an adult.

YOU MAKE THE CALL

As the hearing officer, what would you decide to do with Kimberly? Should she be waived to an adult court for a trial? Or should she be retained in the juvenile court, with renewed efforts to help her with rehabilitation? Write your decision in the space below.

———————————————
———————————————
———————————————
———————————————
———————————————
———————————————

After you have made the call, feel free to go to the appendix and review the decision of the actual court hearing officer in this case. Compare your decision with his and review the rationale for the hearing officer's decision. Then check out the follow-up. What happened to Kimberly in the year following this waiver hearing?

———————————————
———————————————
———————————————

JUVENILE JUSTICE FACT

The current trend among states is to lower the minimum age of eligibility for waiver into adult court. This is due, in part, to the public perception that juvenile crime is on the rise, and offenders are getting younger.

All states except Nebraska, New York, and New Mexico, currently provide for judicial waiver and have set a variety of lower age limits. In most states, the youngest offender who can be waived to adult court is a 17- or 18-year-old, although in some states, this age is as low as 13 or 14. Usually, the offense allegedly committed must be particularly egregious, or there must be a long history of offenses, in order for the case to be waived.

Twenty-eight states have statutory exclusions, which are provisions in the law to exclude some offenses, such as first-degree murder, from juvenile court jurisdiction. Some states also have a legal provision that allows the prosecutor to file a juvenile case in both juvenile and adult courts, because the offense and the age of the accused meet certain criteria.

DESIGNATED PROCEEDINGS OR EXTENDED JURISDICTION JUVENILE PROSECUTIONS

Several states have what are referred to as *designated proceedings*, or *prosecutor-designated cases*, or *extended jurisdiction juvenile proceedings*. When a case is "designated," it means that the juvenile is tried criminally within the juvenile court or within the family court. It is the only kind of juvenile court case that is criminal. However, the juvenile is entitled to all of the protections of the adult criminal court system.

These are cases in which the prosecutor endorses a petition charging a juvenile with a specified juvenile violation with the designation that the juvenile be tried in the juvenile or family court in the same manner as an adult. Usually, each state has a list of juvenile violations that could result in a prosecutor "designating" the case. These violations typically include such offenses as first-degree murder, attempted murder, assault with intent to murder, arson, and kidnapping, as well as several other violations.

INFORMATION YOU SHOULD KNOW

On March 21, 1966, the U.S. Supreme Court decided the case of *Kent v. United States (383 U.S. 541, 86 S. Ct. 1045)*. The background in this case was that in 1961, while on probation from an earlier case, Morris Kent, age 16, was charged with rape and robbery. Kent confessed to the offense as well as to several similar incidents. Assuming that the District of Columbia juvenile court would consider waiving jurisdiction to the adult system, Kent's attorney filed a motion requesting a hearing on the issue of jurisdiction. The juvenile court judge did not rule on this motion filed by Kent's attorney. Instead, he entered a motion stating that the court was waiving jurisdiction after making a "full investigation." The judge did not describe the investigation or the grounds for the waiver. Kent was subsequently found guilty in criminal court on six counts of housebreaking and robbery and sentenced to 30–90 years in prison.

Kent's lawyer sought to have the criminal indictment dismissed, arguing that the waiver had been invalid. He also appealed the waiver and filed a writ of *habeas corpus* asking the state to justify Kent's detention. Appellate courts rejected both the appeal and the writ, refused to scrutinize the judge's "investigation," and accepted the waiver as valid. In appealing to the U.S. Supreme Court, Kent's attorney argued that the judge had not made a complete investigation and that Kent was denied constitutional rights simply because he was a minor.

The U.S. Supreme Court ruled that the waiver was invalid, stating that Kent was entitled to a hearing that measured up to "the essentials of due process and fair treatment," that Kent's counsel should have had access to all records involved in the waiver, and that the judge should have provided a written statement of the reasons for waiver.

The Kent decision actually has a greater impact on juvenile courts than just what appears in the case summary. The Supreme Court raised a potential constitutional challenge to *parens patriae* as the foundation of the juvenile court. In its past decisions, the Supreme Court had interpreted the equal protection clause of the 14th Amendment to mean that certain classes of people could receive less due process if a "compensating benefit" came with this lesser protection. In theory, the juvenile court provided less due process but a greater concern for the interests of the juvenile. The Supreme Court referred to evidence that this compensating benefit may not exist in reality and that juveniles may receive the "worst of both worlds"—"neither the protection accorded to adults nor the solicitous care and regenerative treatment postulated for children."

MORE INFORMATION YOU SHOULD KNOW

The U.S. Supreme Court ruled in another case involving juveniles and waivers in 1975 in *Breed v. Jones (421 U.S. 519, 95 S. Ct. 1779)*. The case started in 1970, when Gary Jones, age 17, was charged with armed robbery. Jones appeared in the Los Angeles juvenile court and was adjudicated delinquent on the original charge and two other robberies. At the dispositional hearing, the judge waived jurisdiction over the case to criminal court. Counsel for Jones filed a writ of *habeas corpus*, arguing that the waiver to criminal court violated the double jeopardy clause of the Fifth Amendment. The court denied this petition, saying that Jones had not been tried twice because juvenile adjudication is not a "trial" and does not place a youth in jeopardy.

Upon appeal, the U.S. Supreme Court ruled that adjudication in juvenile court, in which a juvenile is found to have violated a criminal statute, is equivalent to a trial in criminal court. Thus, Jones *had* been placed in double jeopardy. The Supreme Court also specified that jeopardy applies at the adjudication hearing when evidence is first presented. Waiver cannot occur after jeopardy attaches.

Is it better for the juvenile to be adjudicated in a juvenile court or be waived for trial to an adult court?

The major drawbacks to a juvenile having his or her case heard in a juvenile court are the following ones:

- Juvenile court judges have the power to administer lengthy sentences of incarceration, even for status offenders.
- In most states, a juvenile is unlikely to have a trial by jury in a juvenile court.
- Juveniles do not enjoy the same range of constitutional rights in a juvenile court as adults do in criminal courts.

FOR FURTHER CONSIDERATION

Questions for discussion

1. What are the pros and cons of juveniles bring waived to an adult court?
2. Are juveniles ever competent to be tried as adults? Why or why not?

Review for chapter eleven

Important terms to know:

Waiver hearings: A hearing in the juvenile court to determine if the juvenile should be transferred to an adult court for a criminal trial.

Automatic transfers: Some states have "automatic transfer" laws that require juvenile cases to be transferred to adult criminal court if the offender is a certain age or older (usually 16) and if the charges involve a serious or violent offense.

Competence: The concept of competence in the juvenile court concerns the question: Is the juvenile competent to stand trial? That is, does the juvenile have the ability to function effectively as a defendant in a criminal—or even, for that matter, in a juvenile—proceeding?

Designated proceedings: Several states have what are referred to as *designated proceedings*, or *prosecutor-designated cases*, or *extended jurisdiction juvenile proceedings*. When a case is "designated," it means that the juvenile is tried criminally within the juvenile court or within the family court.

Study guide questions

Choose the right answers from the choices below.

1. In most states, a juvenile offender must be at least 16 to be eligible for waiver to adult court. But, in a number of states, minors as young as 13 could be subjected to a waiver petition. And a few states allow children of
   a. 19 or older to be tried as adults
   b. 21 or older to be tried as adults
   c. 25 or older to be tried as adults
   d. Any age to be tried as adults
2. One of the factors that might lead a court to grant a waiver petition and transfer a juvenile case to adult court involves
   a. The juvenile being charged with a particularly serious offense
   b. The juvenile having several status offenses on his or her record
   c. The minor being younger
   d. Past efforts to rehabilitate the juvenile being successful
3. If the prosecutor or judge seeks to transfer the case to adult court, the minor is entitled to
   a. Financial compensation
   b. A hearing and representation by an attorney
   c. Being allowed to speak in court
   d. A psychiatric evaluation
4. In 2010, juvenile courts waived an estimated _____ delinquency cases, 55% fewer cases than in 1994.
   a. 2,000
   b. 4,000
   c. 6,000
   d. 9,000
5. According to several studies, juveniles waived to adult court are more likely to be
   a. Placed on probation and sent home
   b. Given a medal for valor
   c. Sentenced to community service
   d. Sentenced to prison

chapter twelve

Sentences after a waiver hearing

Sentencing of juveniles

How does a juvenile get sentenced after he or she has been waived to an adult court? The answer to that might seem simple enough. Shouldn't a juvenile who has been waived to an adult court, and subsequently convicted, be sentenced like any other adult?

The answer is no. Because of recent U.S. Supreme Court decisions, juveniles under the age of 18 cannot be sentenced like older adults. Established sentencing guidelines—that would be used in sentencing most adults—do not necessarily apply to juveniles.

In one of the most recent Supreme Court decisions (*Miller v. Alabama*, 2012), the high court ruled that mandatory life sentences without the possibility of parole are unconstitutional for juvenile offenders. This even applies to juveniles convicted of murder.

In an earlier case in 2005, in *Simmons v. Roper*, the Supreme Court declared that juveniles under the age of 18 could not be executed—again, even for murder.

These Supreme Court rulings indicate that those under the age of 18 cannot be sentenced the same way that older adults can be.

Supreme Court decisions

In *Miller v. Alabama (132 S. Ct. 2455)*, the Supreme Court held in 2012 that mandatory sentences of life without the possibility of parole are unconstitutional for juvenile offenders, even if the conviction is for murder. The rulings extended beyond the *Graham v. Florida* (2010) case, which had ruled juvenile sentences of life without parole are unconstitutional for crimes *excluding murder*.

In *Simmons v. Roper (543 U.S. 551)*, the U.S. Supreme Court, on March 1, 2005, held that the 8th and 14th Amendments forbid the execution of offenders who were under the age of 18 when their crimes were committed. In this case, the Supreme Court reaffirmed the necessity of referring to "the evolving standards of decency that mark the progress of a maturing society" to determine which punishments are so disproportionate as to be cruel and unusual. The Supreme Court reasoned that the rejection of the juvenile death penalty in the majority of states, the infrequent use of the punishment even where it remains on the books, and the consistent trend toward abolition of the juvenile death penalty, demonstrated a national consensus against the practice. The Supreme Court determined that today our society views juveniles as categorically less culpable than the average criminal.

Sentencing

If the juvenile is waived to the adult court, tried, and convicted, then he or she is sentenced as an adult.

In other circumstances, such as when the juvenile is tried under designated proceedings, the juvenile judge may retain jurisdiction and could impose both a juvenile and an adult sentence. This is termed a delayed blended sentence and is used in several states. Under the terms of a delayed blended sentence, a convicted youth would serve time in a juvenile facility and be eligible for rehabilitation and therapeutic services there. The adult sentence would be suspended but could be imposed at any time if the defendant committed any of a list of serious or violent offenses while in the juvenile facility or on parole and for a period beyond that. Activation of the adult sentence could mean time in state prison.

Blended sentences

Blended sentences are those that allow courts to impose juvenile or adult sentences on certain juvenile offenders. Twenty-two states allow blended sentences; however, those states vary in terms of which court—the juvenile court or the adult court—has the authority to blend sentences. In effect, blended sentences provide a middle ground between juvenile and adult sentences (Seiter, 2005). The judge can choose from a broad array of both juvenile and adult sanctions—imposing options from both. In some instances, judges may view a blended sentence as giving a juvenile a last chance to benefit from a juvenile sentence. In fact, in many cases, the juvenile is given a juvenile disposition with the understanding that if that disposition is not satisfactorily completed, an adult sentence kicks in; this is the delayed blended sentence. For example, a juvenile might be sentenced to a nine-month residential treatment program in a juvenile facility. If that program is not successful, then the juvenile would be transferred to a state prison for adults.

Sentencing options

In addition to a blended sentence, a judge sentencing a juvenile in an adult court has access to all of the traditional sanctions usually given to adult offenders. These would include probation, jail, prison, fines, and community service. Similarly, a juvenile in an adult court in a few states could be sentenced to all of the usual dispositions for juveniles—residential treatment, probation, restitution, or outpatient treatment.

You make the call in those sentencing cases when a juvenile has been waived to an adult criminal court

You have learned that a waiver hearing is one in which the juvenile court or referee must consider a request to transfer a juvenile to adult court for a trial. You learned in Chapter 11 about the various facts that a hearing officer must take into consideration in order to make the decision as to whether to retain the juvenile in the juvenile court system or transfer him or her to an adult court. The cases presented in this chapter represent two youths who were waived to adult courts. It is now up to you—as the judge in each case—to determine what kind of sentence should be imposed on the juvenile, who is now being sentenced as an adult.

Should the individual be placed on probation? Should he be given a prison sentence? If yes, for how long? What about a blended sentence? Decide what you think is best for each juvenile after reading about his offense and background. Write your decision in the space following each case. Be prepared to state your rationale for your decision and be ready to defend your decision.

The case of Dennis, age 17

Dennis got into trouble just before he turned 17. He was arrested and charged with one count of stolen property, receiving and concealing a stolen motor vehicle, fleeing a police officer, weapons possession, and operating a vehicle without a license. Dennis entered a guilty plea to all of the charges and he was scheduled for sentencing in the adult court.

This is Dennis' first official court involvement, although he has had numerous police contacts over the past few years. For instance, during the past year, Dennis was a suspect in the purchase of crack cocaine and, on three occasions, he was a suspect in the theft of three cars.

When his mother was interviewed by the court caseworker, she said that Dennis and his brother often "tear up the house." She explained that this means they get into fights, break windows, and punch holes in the walls. She described Dennis as her more aggressive and belligerent son, adding that he uses profanity toward her and calls her names. She estimated contacting the police ten or more times asking for help or assistance with him.

Dennis does not attend school, having dropped out shortly after he turned 16. He is not employed, and his mother complains that he does not follow any home rules. He belongs to a local gang, and is often high on marijuana and alcohol. His friends are older than him, and most are in gangs, have been on probation, or have been incarcerated.

Dennis, when talking to the court worker, seemed to have no anxiety or concern about going to court for sentencing. He displayed a rather fatalistic attitude about sentencing, saying that "what will be, will be." He also appeared to have little concern about his reputation in the community, the run-ins he's had with the police, or his future. He said that he has a six-month-old daughter, and he would like to avoid going to prison because he wants to be a "good dad." However, he added that he can't help it if he gets blamed for things. "I do what I have to do," he said, "and if the police don't like me, there's nothing I can do to change that." He said that when he was going to high school, he frequently got into arguments with teachers and was suspended on more than one occasion because of his lack of respect for the principal and assistant principal. He broke school rules and was not interested in working hard to achieve good grades. "It doesn't matter how good you do in school," Dennis told the court worker, "it is a matter of luck what happens to you in the future."

YOU MAKE THE CALL

As the hearing officer, what would you decide to do with Dennis? What kind of sentence should he receive as an adult? Write your decision in the space below.

_____

_____

_____

_____
_____
_____
_____

After you have made the call, feel free to go to the appendix and review the decision of the actual court hearing officer in this case. Compare your decision with his and review the rationale for the judge's decision. Then check out the follow-up. What happened to Dennis in the year following his waiver hearing and sentencing?

_____
_____
_____

The case of James, age 16

James is 16 years old. This is his first time before the court and he is awaiting sentencing in the adult court for one count of armed robbery and one count of assault with intent to rob while armed. He has been in secure detention since the date of the offense, and, at the time of the upcoming sentencing hearing, will have been detained for just over three months. His behavior in detention has been fair.

James stated that he and three friends wanted to go into town, but did not have transportation. One of his friends suggested that they carjack someone. James stated that he really did not want to participate, but said that he was being teased and felt pressured to go along. They all agreed on a plan and started walking toward town. They identified a victim, one of his friends pointed a gun in the window, and James and another boy ran up to the car doors. Both occupants quickly got out of the car, but the boys then changed their minds and only asked for their wallets. James told the court caseworker that he told the two middle-aged occupants to get back in the car and leave, which they did.

Witnesses to this event called the police and uniformed police officers arrived quickly. The boys were still in the vicinity and were stopped for questioning. James denied trying to run away from the police and said that he had, instead, walked up to the patrol car, put his hands in the air, and surrendered. He described the event as a dumb mistake and regrets being a part of it.

James has a troubled home life. His father is serving a life sentence in prison for homicide and multiple counts of armed robbery, and his mother abandoned him before he was a year old. Her whereabouts remains unknown. James was raised by his paternal grandmother, who is involved in his life and very supportive of him. She says that James is a "good boy" and that she has always thought he has the potential for "making something of himself." He follows her rules, helps her out as much as he can at home, and she says that she thought his friends were also good kids.

James is in the 10th grade and is an average student. He was described by his teachers as a quiet student, who attended school regularly, turned in his work, and did just well enough so that he did not stand out as either a very good or very bad student. He has never been suspended, has never been in a fight at school, and most of his teachers said that they would have predicted that he would not be a boy that would get into this kind of trouble.

YOU MAKE THE CALL

As the hearing officer, what would you decide to do with James? What kind of sentence should he receive as an adult? Write your decision in the space below.

_____
_____
_____
_____
_____
_____
_____

After you have made the call, feel free to go to the appendix and review the decision of the actual court hearing officer in this case. Compare your decision with his and review the rationale for the judge's decision. Then check out the follow-up. What happened to James in the year following his waiver hearing and sentencing?

_____
_____
_____

JUVENILE JUSTICE FACTS

At this point in time, there's no extensive research comparing the lengths of prison sentences received by juveniles convicted in criminal courts with those who remained in the juvenile system. What research does indicate that juveniles convicted in adult courts, particularly those convicted of serious or violent offenses, are more likely to be incarcerated and receive longer sentences than juveniles retained in the juvenile system. Despite this, however, they often actually serve only a fraction of the sentences imposed, in many cases less time than they would have served in a juvenile facility.

A 1996 Texas study found that juveniles sentenced in adult court did receive longer terms than they would have received in juvenile court. However, for all offenses except rape, the average prison time actually served was only about 27% of the sentence imposed, in some cases shorter than the possible length of a sentence in a juvenile facility. In a study of the sentences received by youth offenders in New York and New Jersey, researcher Jeffrey Fagan came to similar conclusions. He found that adolescents transferred to adult courts were more likely to be convicted and sentenced to periods of incarceration than those who were adjudicated in the juvenile system. However, all juveniles sentenced to incarceration received nearly identical sentence-length, regardless of whether they were tried in the criminal or the juvenile system.

FOR FURTHER CONSIDERATION

Questions for discussion

1. Should all juveniles convicted in a waiver hearing be sentenced like adults? Why or why not?
2. What are the advantages of the delayed blended sentence?

Review for chapter twelve

Important terms to know:

Blended sentences: Blended sentencing enables courts to impose juvenile or adult correctional sanctions (or both) on certain young offenders.

Delayed blended sentences: The juvenile is given a juvenile disposition with the understanding that if that disposition is not satisfactorily completed, an adult sentence will be imposed.

Study guide questions

Choose the right answers from the choices below.

1. In the case of *Miller v. Alabama* (2012), the U.S. Supreme Court ruled that mandatory life sentences without the possibility of parole
   a. Are just what juveniles need
   b. Are constitutional for juvenile offenders
   c. Are unconstitutional for juvenile offenders
   d. Should be imposed on hardened juvenile offenders
2. In the 2005 case of *Simmons v. Roper*, the U.S. Supreme Court declared that juveniles under the age of 18

   a. Could not be executed—even for murder
   b. Could be executed—if the charge was murder
   c. Could not be executed—even for rape
   d. Could be executed—if the charge was serious enough
3. Under the terms of a delayed blended sentence, a convicted youth would serve time in a juvenile facility and be eligible for rehabilitation and therapeutic services there. The adult sentence would be
   a. Suspended but could be imposed at a later time
   b. Put into action at age 16
   c. Delayed until the juvenile confessed
   d. Suspended, but never imposed
4. In addition to a blended sentence, a judge sentencing a juvenile in adult court has access to all of the traditional sanctions
   a. Usually given to murderers
   b. Usually given to pedophiles
   c. Usually given to young children
   d. Usually given to adult offenders
5. Research indicates that juveniles convicted in adult courts, particularly those convicted of serious or violent offenses, are more likely to be
   a. Placed on probation
   b. Incarcerated and receive longer sentences than juveniles retained in the juvenile system
   c. Placed in the care of a foster home
   d. Incarcerated for a life-term

You make the call in other kinds of juvenile court hearings

chapter thirteen

Violation of probation hearings

Violation of probation

When a youth is placed on probation, the most common requirements include meeting regularly with the juvenile probation officer and obeying all the laws. In addition, the judge or referee may have imposed various other rules and requirements. These may include attending school, obtaining a job, going for counseling, and following the family rules.

If the juvenile fails to comply with the conditions of his or her probation, the juvenile probation officer may initiate a violation-of-probation proceeding. Juvenile probation officers usually have a certain amount of discretion, and if the violation of probation does not involve a new offense—particularly a felony—the probation officer may choose to issue a warning or impose a consequence without a violation-of-probation hearing.

However, if the violation is a serious new offense or if it indicates that probation is not working, a new petition may be filed or the probation officer may request a hearing before the judge or referee.

In general, *violation-of-probation hearings* can be used to promote compliance with the conditions of probation and to support community-based programing.

Violation-of-probation hearings may be initiated in one of two ways:

1. *Filing of a petition:* The juvenile probation officer may initiate a hearing to establish that the juvenile is in violation of the conditions of his or her probation and to allow the court to determine if there is probable cause to hold a hearing.
2. *Probation detention:* Juvenile probation officers have the authority to detain a juvenile probationer and to authorize any law enforcement officer to do so. Once a juvenile is detained, then a probable-cause hearing must be scheduled.

A probable-cause hearing on the detention must be held before a judge or referee within one day. If probable cause is found, the juvenile can be held for a hearing to determine if the juvenile violated one or more conditions of his or her probation. At a probation violation hearing, if the juvenile admits the violation or the court finds that the juvenile violated probation, the court may revoke, modify, or continue probation, and impose any sanctions that could have been imposed at the original disposition hearing. This could include placement out of the home in a residential treatment facility.

During a probation violation hearing, a minor has rights to cross-examine the prosecution's witnesses and the right to call witnesses to challenge the evidence presented by the probation officer or the prosecutor. Hearsay evidence is usually allowed at a probation violation hearing, as long as it is "reliable" in the eyes of the court. Also, the prosecutor only needs to prove by a "preponderance of the evidence" that the child violated probation.

JUVENILE JUSTICE FACT

According to the Office of Juvenile Justice and Delinquency Prevention, probation is the oldest and most widely used community-based corrections program. Probation is used both for first-time, low-risk offenders, and as an alternative to institutional confinement for more serious offenders.

You make the call in these probation violation hearing cases

In this chapter, you have learned that a youth on probation may be returned to court if he or she violates the terms of probation. You have also learned that a probation officer can have a young person taken into custody and detained after the violation of probation rules. If that happens, there must be a hearing to determine if the juvenile will remain in detention or returned home, and to have a probation violation hearing scheduled.

Following are three cases of youths on probation who violated their probation. It is now up to you—as the judge or referee in each case—to determine what kind of plan should be put in place to best help each young person to succeed on probation or make a determination that probation isn't working and a new treatment plan must be implemented.

Should the minor be placed on probation again? Should he or she be given a new order with a new plan? Decide what you think is best for each juvenile in this chapter after reading about their backgrounds and how they came to violate their probation. Write your decision in the space following each case. Be prepared to state your rationale for your decision and be ready to defend your decision.

The case of Steven, age 16

Steven was placed on probation after charges were filed against him for operating a motor vehicle without a license, for delivery and/or manufacture of a controlled substance, and failure to report an accident. He just turned 16 years of age prior to being placed on probation. He is an average student in his high school, and has great potential to play college football. He lives with his mother; his father, who is divorced from his mother, has never been involved in his life. Steven's mother works two jobs to support herself and Steven. When he was placed on probation, the juvenile court referee ordered Steven to complete a nine-month residential treatment program. He successfully completed the program and was released into an aftercare support program. However, within a few weeks he violated the terms of his probation by using marijuana on two occasions. Also, the probation officer, in checking his progress at school, found that he had four unexcused school absences, several unexplained tardies, and had a three-day suspension from school for stealing food from the cafeteria during lunch.

The probation officer assigned him to attend two weekend intervention programs for teens who were violating their probation. But even after these two weekend programs, his suspension from school occurred. The probation officer felt she had no choice but to notify the court that Steven had violated his probation and she was requesting a hearing for a change of plan.

YOU MAKE THE CALL

As the hearing officer, what would you decide to do with Steven? Should he be continued on probation? Or should the plan be changed? If the plan should be changed, what would you recommend? Write your decision in the space below.

_____
_____
_____
_____
_____
_____
_____

After you have made the call, feel free to go to the appendix and review the decision of the actual court hearing officer in this case. Compare your

decision with hers and review the rationale for the judge's decision. Then check out the follow-up. What happened to Steven in the year following this violation of probation hearing?

_____
_____
_____

JUVENILE JUSTICE INFORMATION

Most juvenile dispositions are multifaceted and involve some sort of supervised probation. In 2010, formal probation was the most severe disposition ordered in 61% of the cases in which a youth was adjudicated delinquent.

The case of Christine, age 15

Christine was originally before the court for one count of domestic violence and one count of possession of marijuana. She is 15 years old and lives at home with both parents and two younger brothers. She is in the 10th grade and struggles academically. She admits that she has not put her best effort into her school work. She has also been suspended in the past for being insubordinate and disrespecting her teachers. She was previously on the cheerleading team, but opted out of the current season due to personality conflicts with other girls. She has never participated in counseling or had prior intervention within the community.

Christine was placed on an order for standard probation based on the two charges for domestic violence and possession of marijuana. One of her domestic violence charges grew out of a fight with her mother in which they started off yelling at each other and then slapped each other. The other charge was related to a fight with her 13-year-old brother. Her brother accused her of stealing money from him. She and he argued and she attacked him with a clothes hanger, hitting him on the back and legs with the metal hanger. Within four weeks after being placed on probation, her probation officer discovered that she had failed to follow her probation rules.

Specifically, she was suspended from school twice after arguments with teachers and after swearing at an assistant principal. In addition, she was given a random drug screen and tested positive for marijuana and benzodiazepines. Consequently, her probation officer notified the court that Christine had violated her probation and a change in plan was requested.

YOU MAKE THE CALL

As the hearing officer, what would you decide to do with Christine? Should she be continued on probation? Or should the plan be changed? If you believe the present probation plan is not working, then what would you recommend? Write your decision and recommendations in the space below.

_____
_____
_____
_____
_____
_____
_____

After you have made the call, feel free to go to the appendix and review the decision of the actual court hearing officer in this case. Compare your decision with his and review the rationale for the judge's decision. Then check out the follow-up. What happened to Christine in the year following this probation violation hearing?

_____
_____
_____

The case of Donna, age 14

Donna, age 14, came to the juvenile court on a petition alleging assault and battery. This was her first police contact and first time before the court. The victim of Donna's assault was a teenage girl she knew from school. In a fight after school, Donna hit the other girl approximately a dozen times while the victim was crouched over and defenseless. In an interview with her probation officer, Donna expressed remorse about her actions and stated that as soon as she did it, she knew it was wrong and attempted to apologize.

Donna explained that she was the victim of abuse in the past at the hands of her stepfather. She admits to having a lot of anger and said that she does not speak with anyone

about her frustrations. She added that she would like to participate in counseling and believes that she needs help.

In her disposition hearing, Donna was ordered to attend a day treatment program. She began attending that program, designed to help her learn to deal with emotional problems, especially her anger. However, in the day treatment program, which is held in a local adolescent hospital unit, she failed to follow the program rules. For example, she had four unexcused absences and arrived late to the program three times. Furthermore, she violated probation rules by leaving home without permission when she was on home detention. At school, she was given after-school detention for repeated occurrences of disrespect to teachers, sleeping in class, and using profanity in class. Also, she tested positive for marijuana.

Consequently, her probation officer requested a probation violation hearing, at which time her present probation plan would be reviewed and a change in plan would be considered.

YOU MAKE THE CALL

As the hearing officer, what would you decide to do with Donna? Should she be continued in the day treatment program? Should other parts of the probation plan be changed? If yes, how? What would you recommend? Write your decision in the space below.

_____
_____
_____
_____
_____
_____
_____

After you have made the call, feel free to go to the appendix and review the decision of the actual court hearing officer in this case. Compare your decision with his and review the rationale for the hearing officer's decision. Then check out the follow-up. What happened to Donna in the year following this violation of court order hearing?

_____
_____
_____

JUVENILE JUSTICE PROBATION FACTS

During a period of probation supervision, a juvenile offender remains in the community and can continue normal activities such as school and work. However, the juvenile must comply with certain conditions. This compliance may be voluntary, where the youth agrees to conditions in lieu of formal adjudication. Or compliance may be mandatory, following adjudication, where the youth is formally ordered to a term of probation and must comply with the conditions established by the court. In 920,000 delinquency cases that received a juvenile court sanction in 2010, 53% youths received an order of probation; only 12% of those youths received placement in an out-of-home facility.

In addition to regular meetings with a probation officer, a juvenile may also be required to adhere to a curfew, complete a specified period of community service, or pay restitution. A probation order may also include additional requirements such as drug counseling or weekend confinement in the local detention center. More serious offenders may be placed on intensive supervision requiring more frequent contact with their probation officer and stricter conditions. The term of probation may be for a specified period or may be open-ended. Review hearings are held to monitor the juvenile's progress. After conditions of probation are successfully met, the judge terminates the case. Typically, probation can be revoked if the juvenile violates the probation conditions. If probation is revoked, the court may reconsider its disposition and impose stricter sanctions.

JUVENILE JUSTICE FACTS

There is a fairly high rate of recidivism among youths on standard probation. Across the United States, it is estimated that the recidivism rate is between 40% and 70%. This means that 40%–70% of all juveniles on probation violate their probation. Some studies have suggested that recidivism is related to such factors as the probationer's age, prior criminal offending, having spent time in a residential facility prior to probation, alcohol and drug abuse, poor parental control, school problems, and peer relationship problems. However, it has been shown that recidivism rates are lower when youths are placed in "Intensive Supervised Probation" (ISP) programs.

INTENSIVE SUPERVISED PROBATION

This is a form of probation that generally includes more intensive monitoring by the probation officer. Intensive supervised probation may include, at least at the beginning of probation, home confinement or house arrest, electronic tethering, and other kinds of treatment programs. Many ISP programs require that the probation officer and juvenile have at least three face-to-face meetings per week. In addition, probation officers strictly monitor their school attendance and their participation in community programs, such as drug abuse programs or family counseling sessions. Most ISP programs regularly report lower rates of recidivism as compared to standard probation programs (Champion, 2010).

FOR FURTHER CONSIDERATION

Questions for discussion

1. How much discretion should probation officers have in terms of deciding when to violate or not violate a juvenile's probation?
2. Should more juveniles be placed on intensive probation supervision?

Review for chapter thirteen

Important terms to know:

Probation: Probation is a form of disposition in the juvenile court in which a juvenile offender remains in the community and can continue normal activities such as school and work.

Violation of probation: If the juvenile fails to comply with any condition of probation imposed by the court, he or she can be found to have violated probation, and could be returned to court for a new disposition.

Violation of probation hearing or probation violation hearing: If the juvenile fails to comply with the conditions of his or her probation, the juvenile probation officer may initiate a violation of probation proceeding. In this hearing, the judge or referee may impose a new or more severe sanction.

Intensive probation: A form of probation, often called *intensive supervised probation*, that generally includes more intensive monitoring by the probation officer. Intensive probation may also include, at least at the beginning of probation, home confinement or house arrest, electronic tethering, and other kinds of treatment programs.

Study guide questions

Choose the right answers from the choices below.

1. If the juvenile fails to comply with the conditions of his or her probation, the juvenile probation officer may
   a. Have the juvenile arrested and jailed
   b. Order the juvenile to do community service instead of attending school
   c. Initiate a violation of probation proceeding
   d. Require the juvenile to perform strenuous exercise
2. During a probation violation hearing, a minor has the right to
   a. Ask for a jury
   b. Remain silent
   c. Cross-examine the prosecution's witnesses
   d. Stay away from the hearing
3. Formal probation is generally the disposition ordered in _____ of the cases in which a youth was adjudicated delinquent.
   a. 38%
   b. 61%
   c. 88%
   d. 94%
4. There is a fairly high rate of recidivism among youths on standard probation. Across the United States, it is estimated that the recidivism rate for juveniles is
   a. Between 40% and 70%
   b. Between 10% and 20%
   c. Between 80% and 90%
   d. Between 90% and 95%
5. Most intensive supervised probation programs regularly report _____ rates of recidivism as compared to standard probation programs.
   a. Lower
   b. Higher
   c. Very low
   d. Very high

chapter fourteen

Neglect and abuse hearings

Child abuse and child neglect

Children who are victims of child abuse and neglect come before juvenile and family court judges and referees for protection from further harm, and for timely decision making for their future. Child mistreatment takes place when a parent or caregiver abuses or neglects a child, or allows someone else to abuse or neglect a child. There are several ways an adult could abuse or neglect a child:

- *Physical abuse* includes physical acts that caused or could have caused physical injury to the child, including excessive corporal punishment.
- *Sexual abuse* is involvement of the child in sexual activity either forcefully or without force, including contacts for sexual purposes, prostitution, pornography, or other sexually exploitative activities.
- *Emotional abuse* refers to verbal threats and emotional assaults. It includes terrorizing a child, administering nonprescribed and potentially harmful substances, and willful cruelty or exploitation not covered by other types of maltreatment.
- *Physical neglect* is the disregard of a child's physical needs and physical safety, including abandonment, illegal transfers of custody, expulsion from the home, failure to seek remedial health care or delay in seeking care, or inadequate supervision, food, hygiene, clothing, or shelter.
- *Emotional neglect* includes inadequate nurturing or affection, permitting maladaptive behavior, exposing the child to domestic violence or other maladaptive behaviors or environments, and other inattention to emotional or developmental needs.
- *Educational neglect* includes permitting chronic truancy from school, failure to enroll in school, or other inattention to educational needs.

When children come before juvenile and family court judges and referees for protection, those judges and referees make critical legal decisions, and oversee social service efforts to rehabilitate and maintain families, or to provide permanent alternative care for child victims. Juvenile courts have the responsibility to protect the rights of children as well as parents, while ensuring safe, permanent homes for abused and neglected children.

Among the most important concerns of the juvenile court in neglect and abuse cases, are to see that victims receive treatment, that child abusers receive rehabilitation, that families are preserved as often as possible, and that there is permanency in planning for children. However, in neglect and abuse cases, there are other people and agencies that play roles besides the judge or referee, or the court caseworker. These critical entities include child protection agencies, child therapists, *guardians ad litem*, and attorneys. It is vital that all these major participants play their roles in an effective and responsible manner. But, since what happens to child victims of neglect and abuse depends on the orders of a judge or referee, it is the juvenile court that assumes the responsibility to hold the entire system accountable.

Typically, the first court hearing in a child abuse or neglect case is the preliminary protective hearing. A preliminary protective hearing is referred to in some jurisdictions as a *shelter care hearing, detention hearing, emergency removal hearing,* or *temporary custody hearing.* Such a hearing occurs either immediately before or immediately after a child is removed from home in an emergency. But this initial hearing may take place after a court order that leads to the placement of the child in another home or a program for neglected or abused children. However, in all states, the preliminary protective hearing must take place soon after the child has been removed from his or her home. The main purpose, though, of the preliminary protective hearing, is to make a decision as to whether the child can be immediately and safely returned home while other hearings are scheduled.

As in other juvenile court procedures, in an abuse or neglect case, there is an adjudication hearing in which the court determines whether allegations of abuse or neglect are supported by the evidence, and whether there are legal grounds for the court to intervene on behalf of the child. If the petition seeking court intervention on behalf of a child is supported by the evidence, then the judge or referee may proceed to the disposition stage and determine who shall have responsibility for the child and under what conditions.

Adjudication provides the basis for state intervention into a family, while disposition concerns the nature of such an intervention. In some states, the adjudication hearing is called the *jurisdictional hearing* or *fact-finding hearing.* The outcome of adjudication controls whether the state may intervene, over the objections of the family.

Disposition is the stage of the juvenile court process in which, after finding that the child is within the jurisdiction of the court, the court determines who shall have custody and control of the child. Depending upon the powers and responsibilities of the court under state law, the court may set additional conditions concerning the child's placement, and may issue specific directions to the parties.

Court proceedings to determine disposition are a crucial part of the juvenile court process. At disposition, the court makes the decision whether to remove a child from home, or, if the child is already living elsewhere, whether to continue that out-of-home placement. A full examination of this issue is needed, including an examination of the agency's plan to protect the child from further harm, to prevent placement, and to determine safe alternatives to placement. Based on this examination, the court can then evaluate whether these agency actions constitute reasonable efforts to prevent placement. Dispositional reports and written case plans that address these issues are needed to help the court and parties evaluate the question of removal. When the court decides to place a child outside the home, additional steps are needed to minimize the harm of separation. The court should set terms for appropriate visitation and parent–child communication. The court may need to specify services needed to help the child deal with the trauma of separation, and to deal with the child's other special needs. When the separation of siblings is unavoidable, visitation and communication between siblings must be addressed during disposition.

Decisions at disposition should help the agency and parents develop an appropriate plan to address the specific problems which necessitated state intervention. While adjudication should identify the problems justifying court involvement, disposition should make sure that the parties work out a plan to resolve them. The court should ensure that the agency and court do not work at cross purposes. Disposition should set a framework for review. Effective dispositional proceedings enable review proceedings to evaluate progress in the case. Where the family problems can be clearly described, appropriate services can be identified, and appropriate objectives can be chosen; this will provide a clear focus for subsequent review hearings. The precision with which the needed changes and remedial steps can be identified at disposition, depends on the timing of the disposition hearing, and the nature of the family problems. If the family problems are not yet fully known, the case plan may need to set up further evaluation, rather than to set concrete behavioral goals for parents.

Later, as the case continues, review hearings are scheduled, at which the judge or referee reviews the status of the case. Essentially, the court needs to know if the plan arranged at disposition is being followed. For instance: Are the parents getting help? Is the child in a suitable foster home? Are there steps toward eventual family reunification? Is the permanency plan for the child still viable?

In some abuse and neglect cases, the judge or referee may be considering the termination of parental rights. A hearing would have to be held to hear testimony, and determine if there is sufficient evidence to support the termination of parental rights.

You make the call in these neglect and abuse cases

Following are two cases of minors that have come to the attention of the juvenile court based on allegations of neglect or abuse. The circumstances in each case are somewhat different and they are at different stages of the court process. Read each case closely and make your decision based on the circumstances of the cases. Write your decision in the space following each case. Be prepared to state your rationale for your decision and be ready to defend your decision.

The case of Marissa and her family

The Department of Human Services brought this case to the juvenile court, alleging that the parents of Marissa (15), Mitchell (14), Melanie (4), Emanuel (3), and Amy (2), abused at least one of the children, failed to take the care necessary for the children's health or morals, and subjected the children to a substantial risk of harm to their mental wellbeing, by exposing them to drugs.

Specifically, the following are the reasons the case was brought on a petition to the court:

- On a specific date, Mitchell was hit with a belt buckle by his father and received a large red mark and was cut.
- The mother gave birth to drug-positive infants: Melanie and Emanuel were born positive for marijuana; Amy was born positive for cocaine.
- A search warrant was executed for the parent's home and 3.1 grams of cocaine, a baggie of marijuana, and several marijuana roaches were found. The children were present in the home at the time the warrant was executed.

The father, Roy, is 38 years of age and works at a machine shop where he runs a drill press. He has a high-school education, but has worked at many jobs over the past 20 years, with periods of unemployment from time to time. Roy has a criminal record for possession of cocaine, and for selling marijuana. He denies selling drugs, but admits to using marijuana. He said that he hit Mitchell with a belt because the boy was disrespectful and was not following the rules established by Roy and his wife. In particular, he was skipping classes and lying about what he was doing when he wasn't in school. Roy said he believes he has a right to discipline his children in any way he sees fit.

The mother is Melinda, who is 37. She does not have a high school education, having dropped out at age 17. She has worked from time to time as a bartender, but not in the last year. She has a drug possession charge on her record. She admits that she uses marijuana regularly, but says she stopped using cocaine "about a year ago." She was referred to Narcotics Anonymous, but says she only went once because "I didn't want to talk in front of the losers who went to the group." She says that her husband is not abusive toward the children, but they need a spanking every once in a while.

They are coming into the juvenile court for an adjudication hearing to determine if the parents should be adjudicated as neglectful and/or abusive.

YOU MAKE THE CALL

As the hearing officer, what would you decide to do in this case? Should the parents be adjudicated as abusive, or neglectful, or both? Write your decision in the space below.

_____
_____
_____
_____
_____
_____
_____

After you have made the call, feel free to go to the appendix and review the decision of the actual court hearing officer in this case. Compare your decision with his and review the rationale for the judge or referee's decision. Then check out the

follow-up. What happened in this case in the year following this adjudication hearing?

_____
_____
_____

The case of Andrew and his family

Child Protective Services (CPS) alleges that the children's mother has neglected the children (10-year-old Andrew, 7-year-old Aaron, 4-year-old Stephanie, and 2-year-old Elizabeth) by failing to provide proper support, education, medical, food, and other care necessary for the children's health and welfare. The reasons listed below were given by CPS as to why it is believed that staying with their mother is contrary to their welfare:

- The mother has applied for low-income housing, but remains on a waiting list and such housing is not presently available.
- It has been reported that the family is living on the streets and sleeping in parks.
- The mother's relatives are unable to provide shelter, food, or support for the family.
- The sole source of food for the children has been friends and family providing meals when the mother visits. Those people are unwilling to continue to support the mother and the children.
- None of the children's fathers have provided financial support for the children.
- The mother reports that she is currently pregnant.

In submitting this petition, CPS requested that the court take jurisdiction over the children.

Rachel, age 29, is the mother of these four children, who were removed from her care at a previous hearing and placed in foster care. Each of the children, she told a court caseworker, has a different father, but none of the fathers are involved in seeing the children or helping to support them. Rachel reports that she grew up in a middle-class home in the suburbs of a large city. She graduated from high school and then began to drink heavily and use drugs. When she wasn't going to college, as her parents desired, or working, her parents kicked her out of the home. She began staying with friends, but was drinking heavily. She had her first child when she was 19, and since then has drifted from one city to another.

She states that she has wanted to settle down and raise her children, but she hasn't been able to do that. She admits that her drinking is a problem, and she says that she drinks to deal with her depression. Rachel says she has tried to be a good mother and provide for her kids, but "things just don't work out the way I want them to." She says she loves her children and doesn't want to lose them, but doesn't know how she will manage when she has her next baby. She says that she couldn't go back to her parents' home, because "my mom and dad disowned me a long time ago." She thinks that if she could just get some help she could "turn things around."

YOU MAKE THE CALL

As the hearing officer, what would you decide to do in this case? This is a disposition hearing and in a previous hearing the children were placed in foster care. Should the court terminate the parental rights of Rachel? Or, is there a good plan the court could come up with to keep the family together and make it possible for Rachel to care for her children? Write your decision in the space below.

_____

_____

_____

_____

_____

_____

After you have made the call, feel free to go to the appendix and review the decision of the actual court hearing officer in this case. Compare your decision with hearing officer's, and review the rationale for the judge or referee's decision. Then check out the follow-up. What happened in this case in the year following this disposition hearing?

_____

_____

_____

LEARNING MORE

In 2010, child protective services investigated nearly two million reports of maltreatment involving more than 3.6 million children; 19.5% of these reports were substantiated. Furthermore:

- The 2010 child maltreatment victimization rate of 10.0 per 1000 children under 18 was 25% below the rate in 1990 (13.4 per 1000).
- An estimated 754,000 children were the victims of maltreatment in 2010, down 12% from the number of victims in 1990 (860,000).

Neglect is by far the most common form of maltreatment; in 2010, 78% of victims experienced neglect. This was followed by physical abuse (18%) and sexual abuse (9%).

The vast majority of perpetrators were parents (81%), including birth parents, adoptive parents, and step-parents. The unmarried partner of the parent was the perpetrator in 2.5% of the cases, and a friend or neighbor was the perpetrator in only 0.3% of instances.

JUVENILE JUSTICE FACTS

Seven years after the U.S. Supreme Court issued its landmark decision in *In re Gault*, the courts extended the right to representation to children in child protection cases with the creation of the *guardian ad litem* (GAL) requirement with the passage of the Child Abuse Prevention and Treatment Act of 1974 (CAPTA). As passed by Congress, CAPTA provided federal funding to states in support of prevention, assessment, investigation, prosecution, and treatment activities, and also provided grants to public agencies and nonprofit organizations for demonstration programs and projects. Additionally, CAPTA identified the Federal role in supporting research, evaluation, technical assistance, and data collection activities; established the Office on Child Abuse and Neglect; and mandated the National Clearinghouse on Child Abuse and Neglect Information.

But, CAPTA also required that states seeking federal funds must appoint *guardian ad litems* to represent children in proceedings related to child abuse, neglect, or dependency (Houston and Barton, 2005).

FOR FURTHER CONSIDERATION

Questions for discussion

1. Under what circumstances should a parent's right to care for and raise a child or children be terminated?
2. How should juvenile courts best protect vulnerable children from neglect and abuse?

Review for chapter fourteen

Important terms to know:

Physical abuse: Physical abuse includes physical acts that caused or could have caused physical injury to the child, including excessive corporal punishment.

Sexual abuse: Sexual abuse is involvement of the child in sexual activity either forcefully or without force, including contacts for sexual purposes, prostitution, pornography, or other sexually exploitative activities.

Guardian ad litem: A person the court appoints to represent the best interests of a child in a juvenile court case.

Study guide questions

Choose the right answers from the choices below.

1. A preliminary protective hearing is referred to in some jurisdictions as a "shelter care hearing," "detention hearing," "emergency removal hearing," or "temporary custody hearing;" however, such a hearing occurs
   a. When a child is declared a delinquent
   b. When a child is waived to an adult court
   c. When a child is placed on probation
   d. Either immediately before or immediately after a child is removed from home in an emergency
2. In 2010, child protective services investigated nearly two million reports of maltreatment involving
   a. Less than one million children
   b. About 500,000 children
   c. More than 3.6 million children
   d. More than 10 million children
3. The most common form of maltreatment of children is
   a. Neglect
   b. Sexual abuse
   c. Spanking
   d. Emotional abuse
4. The Child Abuse Prevention and Treatment Act of 1974 established
   a. The Office on Child Abuse and Neglect
   b. The Drug Enforcement Agency
   c. The Office of Wayward Children
   d. The Central Intelligence Agency

chapter fifteen

Review hearings

Review hearings

Typically, juvenile courts are required to hold review hearings at least every six months. There are numerous options for the judge or referee at a review hearing. At the review hearing, the hearing officer will have a report from the probation officer or the court caseworker, and, in addition, there may be reports from the prosecutor, the parents or guardians, and the child. While the probation officer will have submitted a written progress report, other reports may be oral or informal.

If the child is making good progress, the hearing officer can continue the juvenile on probation, modify the previous plan, or dismiss the case. If the child is in out-of-home care, the court could continue to maintain the child in out-of-home care and continue family reunification services, or return the child to a parent. If the child has not made adequate progress, the hearing will resemble the violation of probation hearing, which was discussed in Chapter 13.

Review hearings could be held every few months for a year or longer. In some instances, young people remain on probation for several years—although this is the exception rather than the rule. However, no matter what, juvenile court jurisdiction must end at age 21. Depending on the age that a particular state sets for juvenile jurisdiction to end (it may be 17 or 18 in a majority of states), most young people who come into the juvenile justice system will be dismissed by that age.

Whether a juvenile has been on probation or incarcerated, there will still be regular court hearings to review his or her progress. When the probation officer or court caseworker believes that he or she has made sufficient progress, a termination hearing will be requested. On the other hand, when a young person has reached the age of juvenile court termination—again, that will be age 17 or 18 in most states—and if they are continuing to get into trouble, the juvenile court may dismiss the case with the understanding that they will "graduate" into the adult system.

When the caseworker or probation officer takes a youth back to court for the termination or dismissal hearing, they will present a report recommending dismissal from juvenile court jurisdiction. It will, though, be up to the judge or referee to make the final decision for termination from the court's jurisdiction.

JUVENILE JUSTICE FACTS

The National Council of Juvenile and Family Court Judges encourages judges to schedule reviews more frequently than the law requires, which is usually every six months. By having more frequent review hearings, juvenile courts may expedite the resolution of cases, address an unresolved issue, monitor parent or agency compliance with a court directive, or respond to a party's motion (that could be from the prosecutor or a defense attorney).

You make the call in these review hearing cases

The case of Thomas, age 16

Thomas, age 16, was placed on a standard probation order because he was charged in a petition from his high school with school truancy.

Prior to coming to juvenile court, Thomas, a 10th grade student, lived with his mother. His parents are divorced, and he was seeing his father regularly. However, after being placed on probation, Thomas asked the probation officer if he could move from his mother's house to his dad's house. He said that he thought the lack of rules and supervision at his mother's house was a contributing factor in his truancy from school. The probation officer agreed to try this.

His father had much higher expectations of Thomas and was better at holding him accountable for his behavior. His father provided closer supervision, making sure he got up for school on time and seeing to it that he actually arrived at school. This has likely been an important factor in Thomas' success on probation. One month, when his father was going to be out of town on a business trip, Thomas went back to his mother's for two weeks. During the two weeks he was back with his mother, he missed three days of school. That resulted in a consequence imposed by the court, which was a work weekend at the local juvenile detention facility.

Immediately following the weekend, Thomas returned to his father's home. From that point on, there were no absences from school. His probation officer met with him consistently over the next six months of his probation—often showing up unannounced at school to see him. He always located Thomas and found him in school, in good spirits, and with the necessary school supplies. Since the weekend work project, his attendance has been excellent, and his grades have shown an improvement over the previous year.

At the review hearing, his probation officer reported that Thomas had grown used to getting up every morning, getting on the bus, and attending school. Thomas assured the probation officer that he plans to continue to be a good student who attends school every day. As part of his probation, Thomas wrote an essay regarding the importance of education and what he has learned from his court experience. It was a well-written essay that expressed his desire to improve as a student and as a person. He wrote that he learned that self-discipline was very important to continued success in life. Thomas also completed several random drug screens, all of which were clean.

YOU MAKE THE CALL

As the hearing officer, what would you decide to do with Thomas? Should he be continued on probation or should other plans be made? Should he be dismissed from the court? Write your recommendations and decisions in the space below.

_____
_____
_____
_____
_____
_____

After you have made the call, feel free to go to the appendix and review the decision of the actual court hearing officer in this case. Compare your decision with his, and review the rationale for the judge's or referee's decision. Then check out the

follow-up. What happened to Thomas in the year following this review hearing?

_____
_____
_____

The case of Katrina, age 16

Katrina originally came to the court for two counts of assault and battery and one count of possession of marijuana. Her last hearing was a review hearing held three months ago. At that time, she was almost finished with a residential treatment program. The court continued her in the program and scheduled another review in three months. The matter is now back before the court for that review.

Katrina successfully completed her program and was released to both parents two months ago. She made remarkable progress throughout her nine-month residential treatment program. She appeared to gain great insight into her past poor behaviors and the negative path she had been on. She developed a strong motivation to do well in life and she left the program focused on working hard to reach her goals. In the two months since she has been back at home, she has maintained a positive attitude and shown that she has a sincere desire to do well in all areas of her life.

Throughout her residential program, she participated in family therapy, individual therapy, and group therapy with peers in the program. She became a leader in her group therapy, and successfully completed the program's Moral Reconation Therapy. (Moral Reconation Therapy is an important cognitive-behavioral program for substance abusers and juvenile offenders.) Katrina also completed a 21-day intensive substance abuse treatment program, participated in several community service projects, and volunteered throughout the summer with a therapeutic horseriding program for young people with disabilities.

Since her release and her return home, Katrina has continued to do well. She now attends a local high school where she is completing her junior year. Her probation officer has visited her at school several times and has always found her to be present and in good spirits. Teachers and staff at her school have noted the positive changes that she has made, and have reported that she has been diligent about getting to class on time and associating with a positive peer group. Katrina has studied for and taken the ACT (the academic readiness for college test) and is currently awaiting her score. Her goal is to graduate from high school and attend college.

In the last two months, she has completed four random drug screens, all of which have shown she is clean of drugs. Her father has consistently reported that Katrina is changed at home. She is polite and respectful, and helpful with household chores. Katrina has also become a mentor, providing emotional support for her older brother, who is struggling with mental health difficulties.

Katrina has tried very diligently to find a part-time job; however, she has not found a job yet. She has applied at many local fast-food restaurants and grocery stores. She makes follow-up visits and phone calls, and still remains hopeful of finding a job for the summer between her junior and senior years. She also plans to complete driver's education this next summer.

In summary, Katrina appears to have made a successful transition home and back into the community. However, she has only been at home and in her community high school for two months, but the indications are, according to her probation officer, that she will continue to be successful.

YOU MAKE THE CALL

As the hearing officer, what would you decide to do with Katrina? Should she be continued on probation or should other plans be made? Should she be dismissed from the court? Write your decision in the space below.

_____
_____
_____
_____
_____
_____

After you have made the call, feel free to go to the appendix and to review the decision of the actual court hearing officer in this case. Compare your decision with his and review the rationale for the judge's decision. Then check out the follow-up.

What happened to Katrina in the year following this review hearing?

_____
_____
_____

The case of Sarah, age 16

Sarah was placed on a standard probation order after appearing in court on charges of credit card theft and possession of a weapon. She is now returning to court for a six-month review.

Sarah lives with her mother, who has consistently reported that Sarah's home behavior is exemplary. Her mother believes that being on probation with the juvenile court has been a positive learning experience for Sarah.

Sarah is currently just over seven months pregnant. She has been faithful in maintaining consistent prenatal care and following through with all of her doctor's recommendations. Additionally, she receives home-based support from a public health nurse and a nutritionist, both of whom visit with her between one and two times a month. At these visits, Sarah has been learning about the stages of her pregnancy, the baby's development, childbirth, breastfeeding, and general parenting skills.

Sarah began her probation attending a traditional high school. However, due to her pregnancy, she transferred to an alternative high school program that offers a much smaller, quieter school setting where students work individually on computer-based classes. Sessions are 4 h long and students elect whether to attend in the morning or afternoon. Sarah attends morning sessions, which appears ideal for her at this time. She has maintained near-perfect attendance and has been working hard in her classes. As she progresses in her pregnancy and after the baby is born, she will be able to complete schoolwork online from home.

Sarah has done well complying with her probationary goals. She has completed four random drug screens, all of which have been clean. She tried to find part-time employment, but has been unsuccessful. In her alternative high school program, she is completing youth community service with the Red Cross, where she checks donors in, and feeds them juice and cookies after they donate blood. She is interested in pursuing a career in the nursing field, which has made her volunteer job with the Red Cross an especially beneficial experience.

Sarah has successfully complied with the court's requirements, with the exception of getting a job. However, she has put forth an effort to obtain a part-time job. She is doing well in all phases of her life; she has been working hard in school, maintaining consistent prenatal care, and is focused on a positive lifestyle. Her mother is very involved in Sarah's life and provides great support. Sarah will turn 17 within a month after this review hearing. She is well aware that she will go to an adult court after she turns 17, should she re-offend. She has assured her probation officer that she has learned a great lesson and will stay on a positive path.

Although Sarah's progress and behavior have been positive, there are still several high-risk factors. These include her teen pregnancy, new responsibilities and roles once her baby arrives, recent changes in her school plan, and attendance at an alternative high school, and her previous history of drug use.

YOU MAKE THE CALL

As the hearing officer, what would you decide to do with Sarah? Should she be continued on probation or should other plans be made? Should she be dismissed from the court? Write your decision in the space below.

_____

_____

_____

_____

_____

_____

After you have made the call, feel free to go to the appendix and to review the decision of the actual court hearing officer in this case. Compare your decision with his, and review the rationale for the judge's decision. Then check out the follow-up. What happened to Sarah in the year following this review hearing?

_____

_____

_____

FOR FURTHER CONSIDERATION

Questions for discussion

1. If a juvenile has been living apart from his or her parents, should the juvenile court always pursue family reunification plans? Why or why not?
2. If a juvenile is doing well on probation, might there be an argument for continuing probation for, say, another three months?

Review for chapter fifteen

Important terms to know:

Review hearing: A juvenile court hearing to monitor the progress of a juvenile.
Family reunification: Based on the assumption that children are better off if raised by their natural parents, family reunification seeks to reunite children with their parents when separation has occurred.

Study guide questions

Choose the right answers from the choices below.

1. Typically, juvenile courts are required to hold review hearings at least every
   a. Month
   b. Three months
   c. Six months
   d. Twelve months
2. If the juvenile is making good progress, the hearing officer can, at his or her review hearing, continue the juvenile on probation, modify the previous plan, or
   a. Dismiss the case
   b. Send the juvenile to foster care
   c. Place the child in a detention facility
   d. Refer the juvenile to a social agency
3. When the caseworker or probation officer takes a juvenile back to court for the termination or dismissal hearing, he or she will present a report recommending dismissal from juvenile court jurisdiction. However, it will be up to the _____ to make the final decision for termination from the court's jurisdiction.
   a. Parents
   b. *Guardian ad litem*
   c. Judge or referee
   d. Prosecuting attorney
4. The National Council of Juvenile and Family Court Judges encourages judges to schedule review hearings more frequently than
   a. Every month
   b. Every six months
   c. Every year
   d. The law requires

chapter sixteen

Drug courts

Specialty courts, such as teen courts, gun courts, and drug courts, provide alternatives to the formal juvenile court system. While specialty courts target specific offenders—for example, those who used a gun in an offense or those who use illicit drugs—they are operated both in adult courts as well as in juvenile courts or family courts.

Juvenile drug courts have only been around since about 1995, but their popularity has increased markedly since then. Although there are close to 3000 drug courts in the United States, approximately 2000 of those courts are designed for juveniles (Taylor and Fritsch, 2011).

Typically, youth petitioned to the juvenile court because of the alleged violation of a drug law may be diverted to the drug court—if one is available in the juvenile or family court where the young person resides. Often, the juvenile must not be accused of or adjudicated for the commission of a violent offense. However, once accepted into the drug court, the minor will be required to come to a court hearing weekly for progress hearings.

In the drug court, the juvenile will be required to participate in drug treatment while being subjected to strict monitoring by the probation officer and the drug court.

Drug court hearings are usually very informal, with support offered to each individual by the judge and the staff as well as other participants. Drug court participants are usually offered incentives to kick their drug habit and to continue to meet the stringent requirements of the drug court. At the end of their stint in drug court—which can be as long as a year or more—juveniles who are successful are offered a joyous graduation ceremony to celebrate their progress.

Research has found that drug courts provide closer, more comprehensive supervision and much more frequent drug-testing and monitoring than other forms of probation and community supervision. As a result, studies conclude that recidivism rates for drug-court graduates are as much as two to four times lower than for those who do not participate in drug courts (Taylor and Fritsch, 2011).

One other advantage of juvenile drug courts, and perhaps an additional reason for their success, is the fact that most juvenile drug courts emphasize family functioning and the integration of the family into the treatment process.

Typically, judges who head up juvenile drug courts volunteer for the assignment and take on this role—which often means night court hearings to accommodate juveniles and their families, allowing them to attend weekly hearings together—with enthusiasm for the program and a willingness to help rehabilitate adolescent drug abusers.

You make the call in those juvenile drug cases when a juvenile has been referred to the drug court

You have learned that a juvenile drug court hearing is one in which the juvenile drug court judge must consider the background and circumstances of a juvenile in order to decide the best course of treatment for the young person. The cases presented in this chapter represent two youths who were referred to the juvenile drug court. It is now up to you—as the judge in each case—to determine what kind of treatment disposition should be imposed on the juvenile.

Should the individual receive residential or outpatient drug treatment? What other conditions should be imposed on him or her? Decide what you think is best for each juvenile after reading about their respective offenses and backgrounds. Write your decision in the space following each case. Be prepared to state your rationale for your decision and be ready to defend your decision.

The case of Dian, age 16

Dian was 16 when she was identified as a candidate for the juvenile drug court program. She had several offenses for minor in possession of alcohol, which is what brought her to the juvenile court. Although she had tried other drugs, such as marijuana and prescription pills, alcohol was her drug of choice.

She grew up in a family in which there was a strong family history of alcoholism. Her father was well known in the local legal community as a respected defense attorney. He was a single parent, as Dian's mother died from of complications from her own alcohol addiction when Dian was in the fourth grade. Additionally, there were at least three family members—an aunt, an uncle on her father's side, and a grandfather—all of whom had died from cirrhosis, suicide, and other complications of late-term addictions.

Dian was a short, mild-mannered, and quiet teenager, but when she drank she would become aggressive and belligerent. Furthermore, when she started drinking, she couldn't stop, and would drink such excessive amounts that she had nearly died from alcohol poisoning three different times. She told the drug court caseworker who interviewed her that she now realized she had an alcohol problem because she was hospitalized for alcohol poisoning. She assured the caseworker that she could stop drinking.

The girl attended a Catholic high school where she received above average grades and was well liked by other students and teachers. She was frequently invited to parties, and always had fun, although it was at those parties that she tended to drink excessively. She confided to the caseworker that it was at a party when she was 15 that she was raped by a boy she knew. She never told her father or her school counselor because she felt too ashamed.

Dian began drinking at age nine when she got into her father's liquor cabinet, and also drank some of her father's beer from the refrigerator. She found that she could consume large quantities of beer or scotch without appearing to be drunk. When she started to go to parties at age 13, she got a reputation for being able to "hold" her alcohol and drink more than the boys at the parties. She said that she could not remember how many times she had been drunk in her life.

Her father fit the criteria for an alcoholic, although he said that he only drank "socially." He admitted that he usually drank a "few beers" after work, often stopping at a bar or a restaurant to meet friends or business associates. He also said that he had one or more alcoholic drinks—often a scotch and soda—for lunch at least three times a week. He denied that his drinking was problematic or that it was connected to Dian's use of alcohol. He told the caseworker that "I never drink around Dian except for a beer or two at night." Dian, on the other hand, said that she frequently saw him drink at parties, restaurants, and in his office at home.

Dian said that all of her high-school friends drank beer and used marijuana, although she didn't think that she was influenced by the drug and alcohol use of her friends.

YOU MAKE THE CALL

As the judge, what would you decide to do with Dian? What kind of treatment recommendations should she receive? Write your decision in the space below.

_____
_____
_____
_____
_____
_____

After you have made the call, feel free to go to the appendix and review the decision of the actual juvenile drug court judge in this case. Compare your decision with his and review the rationale for the judge's decision. Then check out the follow-up. What happened to Dian in the year following her first appearance in juvenile drug court?

_____
_____
_____

The case of Jackson, age 17

Jackson was 17 when he was identified for the juvenile drug court. He was older than the typical drug court participant, but had come into the juvenile court at 16 and the court decided to extend the court's jurisdiction beyond age 17 because of his heroin addiction.

Jackson is a heroin user who injects heroin intravenously (IV). He first came to the juvenile court on a petition from the police after he was involved in a drug-fueled episode in which he stole a car from a parking lot and crashed into a police car.

He lives with both of his parents in a wealthy part of the county. His father is a surgeon and his mother an advertising professional. Jackson is the older of two boys in the family. Jackson attended one of the best public high schools in the county and was an outstanding student. However, his grades have been declining for two years, and the drug court caseworker believed that the decline was a result of his increasing use of heroin and his addiction.

He said that he was first introduced to heroin when he was in the ninth grade, when he was at a party in a friend's house. Jackson came to high school with outstanding promise as a baseball player; the party was put on by a teammate, and all of the junior varsity—and some of the varsity players—were at the party. He saw some of the varsity players he admired using heroin and he thought he would try it because it seemed safe if good athletes were using it. He liked the high he got from it and continued to use it. He said he was certain that he could use it occasionally without getting addicted to heroin.

By the time he was 15, he was hooked on heroin and he had to constantly try to come up with enough money to buy heroin. He sold marijuana to other kids at school for a time, but he was caught and suspended. His parents and the vice-principal at school thought that it was a simple case of a student selling a little bit of marijuana to his friends and didn't see it as a serious issue—although it caused his suspension. As his struggle to support his habit continued, he had to find other ways to get money.

He shoplifted from department stores, pulled an unarmed robbery at a convenience store, and then got involved in male prostitution by age 16. At one point, he was prostituting with an older man, who was arrested with Jackson in a city park. The man was charged with child sexual abuse in a widely publicized trial. Though Jackson was never identified in the media, many of his classmates were aware that he was the victim in the case. Every time there was a news story related to the case, life became more difficult for Jackson. He continued using heroin, and when this case was scheduled for the juvenile drug court, Jackson was being considered for transfer to an alternative high school for students with academic and behavioral problems.

Jackson's parents were concerned about their son and indicated their cooperation in getting him help through the juvenile drug court.

YOU MAKE THE CALL

As the drug court judge, what would you decide to do with Jackson? What kind of program would you order for him? Write your decision in the space below.

_____
_____
_____
_____
_____
_____
_____

After you have made the call, feel free to go to the appendix and review the decision of the actual drug court judge in this case. Compare your decision with his, and review the rationale for the judge's decision. Then check out the follow-up. What happened to Jackson in the year following his entrance into drug court?

_____
_____
_____

FOR FURTHER CONSIDERATION

Questions for discussion

1. Why are drug courts so successful?
2. Is it possible that the informality of juvenile drug courts is a reason for their success?

Review for chapter sixteen

Important terms to know:

Drug courts: Specialty courts designed to help people who have problems with drugs and alcohol.

Study guide questions

Choose the right answers from the choices below.

1. Drug courts have only been around since 1989, but their popularity has _____ since then.
   a. Decreased
   b. Stayed about the same
   c. Increased
   d. Increased markedly
2. Approximately _____ drug courts in this country are designed for juveniles.
   a. 500
   b. 1000
   c. 2000
   d. 5000

3. In order to be eligible to participate in a juvenile drug court, the juvenile must not be accused of or adjudicated for the commission of a
   a. Violent offense
   b. Sexual offense
   c. Drug offense
   d. Shoplifting offense
4. Research concludes that recidivism rates for drug court graduates are as much as _____ times lower than for those who do not participate in drug courts.
   a. One to two
   b. Two to four
   c. Five to seven
   d. Eight to ten

section six

Appeals and the last word

chapter seventeen

Appeals of juvenile court cases

Just like adults, juveniles may appeal an adjudication or disposition. The reason for this is that the right to appeal is an integral part of the criminal justice process. Nowhere in the Constitution does it state that criminal defendants have the right to an appeal, however; it is a right given to defendants by law in all states (del Carmen and Trulson, 2006). This is the case in both adult criminal cases and juvenile cases.

Unlike adults, juveniles do not have a constitutional right to bail before, during, or after trial. The courts have not granted this set of rights to juveniles. Therefore, if a juvenile is appealing his or her adjudication or disposition, there is no absolute right to bail pending the outcome of the appeal. However, the release of a juvenile while an appeal is ongoing is governed by state law, and state court decisions and practices vary from state to state (del Carmen and Trulson, 2006).

Habeas corpus

Juveniles do have the right to file a writ of *habeas corpus*. A writ of *habeas corpus* is a writ directed at any person who is detaining a juvenile, and it directs that person (say, the director of a juvenile detention facility or a state training school) to produce the body (*corpus*) of the individual and explain why detention is justified.

There are differences between an appeal and a writ of *habeas corpus*. An appeal is part of the criminal proceeding, while a writ of *habeas corpus* is a separate civil proceeding after the criminal case. The purpose of an appeal is to reverse the adjudication (or conviction), while the purpose of a writ of *habeas corpus* is to secure release from an institution. Also, appeals must be filed within a certain time period, and a writ of *habeas corpus* may be filed at any time as long as the juvenile is detained. And, finally, a major difference between an appeal and a writ of *habeas corpus* is that an appeal must raise issues from the trial record with no new evidence allowed, whereas a writ of *habeas corpus* may present new evidence (del Carmen and Trulson, 2006).

FOR FURTHER CONSIDERATION

Questions for discussion

1. Should juveniles have the right to appeal their adjudications in a juvenile court?

2. Should juveniles have a right to bail if they have been detained and they are appealing their detention?

Review for chapter seventeen

Important terms to know:

Appeal: The process by which a defendant asks a higher court to review the decision of a lower court.

Bail: A means of securing the release of an individual who is detained. Usually some form of security is provided to the court in order to assure that the individual will appear for future court hearings.

Habeas corpus: A writ of *habeas corpus* is a writ directed at any person who is detaining a juvenile; it directs that person to explain why detention is justified.

Study guide questions

Choose the right answers from the choices below.

1. Juveniles may appeal an adjudication or
   a. A social history report
   b. A detention at school
   c. A disposition
   d. An unfavorable deposition
2. Juveniles do not have a constitutional right to _____ before, during, or after trial.
   a. An attorney
   b. A *guardian ad litem*
   c. Free speech
   d. Bail
3. Juveniles do have the right to file a
   a. Writ of *habeas corpus*
   b. Writ of *mandamus*
   c. Writ of *certiorari*
   d. Writ of assistance

chapter eighteen

Wrapping it up

In this book, we have provided a brief description of the juvenile justice process, along with a history of how juvenile courts were developed in the United States. You also learned about the constitutional rights juveniles have in juvenile courts, and you learned that minors can be waived to adult criminal courts. Then, we gave descriptions of the most common kinds of juvenile court hearings. You have had a chance to read some court cases and offer your own ideas and recommendations for what should happen to the juveniles represented in those cases.

As you learned, dealing with juvenile court cases is not easy. A juvenile court judge or referee has to take into consideration many factors. Always, when dealing with minors, there is an awesome responsibility that comes with each case. A juvenile court case is not simply an offense or a case number. Each one is a person and the hearing officer's obligation is to keep that in mind as he or she decides the fate of a young person. In an adult court, perhaps judges can rationalize their decisions and court orders by believing that the individual offender has made life decisions and choices with a mature mind, a mind capable of weighing all of the options and consequences. In the case of children and adolescents, however, we are all much more aware these days that the young person's brain and thinking processes are still immature, malleable, and capable of change. In other words, the young mind of a child or adolescent is still unformed. Decisions—including court orders—that affect a young life can have profound long-term effects on a juvenile's future.

Therefore, hearing officers can never take their job lightly or afford to be jaded or cynical. Every day, a judge or referee has an opportunity to influence a youth so that person can be helped to make better choices in the future.

This book, we hope, has given you an introduction to the kinds of decisions that must be made in a juvenile court. However, if you plan to work with juveniles, even if you never become a judge or referee, you will want to learn all that you can about the growth and development of children and adolescents. Furthermore, criminal justice classes, and courses on juvenile justice or juvenile delinquency, will help you gain an overall understanding of the justice system and how it has developed to meet the needs of minors while at the same time protecting the safety of society. But we urge you to also take child psychology and child development classes to learn more about the way children develop and the kinds of expectations adults should have for children and teens at every stage of development.

There will be no substitute, however, for spending time with children—watching them grow, develop, and interact with one another. Nor is there any better way to learn about the juvenile justice system than to observe actual juvenile court hearings with experienced judges and referees.

Finally, we encourage you to continue to learn as much as you can about the juvenile justice system. While it is not a perfect system, it is the system we use in this country. As you discovered in Chapter 5, there are several important players in a juvenile court hearing. No matter which role you might play in the future in the juvenile justice system, our hope is that you can contribute to the system to make it even better than it is today and that you continue to work to improve the lives of young people.

Appendix

Chapter seven: Decisions at intake

The case of Brody

1. *The referee's decision:* The referee placed Brody on the consent docket with a six-month review. He was ordered to continue with psychiatric treatment as well as intensive, home-based individual and family counseling. Brody was also ordered to complete 25 h of youth community service and write a detailed essay regarding his offense, how he will handle situations differently in the future, and his plan for continued improvement.

2. *The referee's rationale:* The referee gave weight to the fact that this was Brody's first time before the court and that he had made notable improvements since the date of the offense; that he had an extensive mental health history, and was fully engaged with all services at the time of disposition. Brody was doing well in his new school. He was following all school rules and seeking the support of school officials when necessary. His progress could be easily monitored by the court regardless of the type of probation the referee ordered. Therefore, there was little risk in allowing him the opportunity to earn "consent" status (avoid having a formal record) because any failures to comply would result in him being returned to court to revoke consent and consider a more restrictive plan.

3. *What happened to Brody:* Brody successfully completed all consent probation requirements, continued to do well in therapy and had no additional police contacts or behavior concerns. Therefore, the matter was closed in six months. Unfortunately, two months later, he was adjudicated on a new petition for false report or threat of terrorism. He was placed in secure juvenile detention and later moved to a residential treatment program that will focus on mental health treatment, behavior modification, individual and family therapy, and academic improvement. These types of programs typically take six to nine months to complete before the juveniles are returned home.

The case of Makayla

1. *The referee's decision:* The referee decided to place her on the consent docket with a six-month review. She ordered that Makayla be restricted to home, school, and scheduled appointments immediately upon her release. Makayla was placed on 30 days of home detention, monitored by a tether. She was ordered to return to individual and family counseling services immediately. Her mother was ordered to participate fully as well. Makayla was ordered to follow all home rules, have only restricted contact with friends, and have limited use of her cellphone. Random drug screens were ordered, along with an essay regarding her crime, including what she has learned and how her behavior has affected others.

2. *The referee's rationale:* The referee gave great consideration to Makayla being only 13 years old and that it was her first offense. The referee felt that family counseling services were most important and should help them begin to repair their relationship. Submitting to random drug screens would encourage Makayla to remain clean, and writing an essay regarding her crime would force her to reflect on her actions and gain a better understanding of the many consequences of her behavior. An important factor considered by the referee was that Makayla's mother, who was the victim of her crime, requested that Makayla be released from juvenile detention and returned home on probation. She noted that if Makayla failed to follow the rules of consent probation, she would schedule Makayla for early review hearing to consider revoking her consent status and placing her on a formal probation order or possibly something more restrictive.

3. *What happened to Makayla:* Makayla failed her consent probation by leaving home without permission, being suspended from school and failing to provide a usable drug screen sample. She was returned to court, placed in secure juvenile detention for three weeks and released on a formal,

more intensive probation order. Makayla remains on probation to date. She is in full compliance and will likely be released from the juvenile court's jurisdiction within the next two months. However, she now has a formal adjudication for domestic violence on her record.

Chapter eight: Initial hearings

The case of Jamie

1. *The hearing officer's decision:* Jamie was appointed legal counsel at the initial hearing. After a short consultation, she pled guilty to the retail fraud charge. The referee scheduled the matter for a formal disposition hearing three weeks later and held Jamie in secure detention during the interim.
2. *The hearing officer's rationale:* The referee based his decision to continue to hold Jamie in detention based on her poor attitude and extremely disrespectful demeanor toward all authority figures in her life—her parents, school officials, loss prevention officers, and the police. The referee also noted Jamie's failure to take responsibility for her behaviors—not just for the theft, but also for her school troubles and difficulties at home. It was determined that a brief period of confinement in detention would provide her with time to reflect on her life and perhaps take greater responsibility for herself in the future and learn to display a more appreciative and positive attitude.
3. *What happened to Jamie:* Jamie was ultimately placed on a formal probation order that was reviewed after six months. She attended weekly counseling sessions, completed 40 h of youth community service, toured the local women's jail, and wrote an essay regarding the effects of retail fraud and what she has learned from her experience. She maintained good school attendance and also improved her behavior at home. She was released from probation at the six-month review hearing and to date, she has not reoffended.

The case of David

1. *The hearing officer's decision:* The referee authorized David's case for a formal juvenile court hearing and ordered that he continue in secure detention at the local juvenile detention center.
2. *The hearing officer's rationale:* The referee gave great consideration to a number of factors: the seriousness of the crime—it was a second weapons offense, and the gun was loaded, placing himself and several others at great risk; David's behavior had not improved despite the previous year of rehabilitative services; and that he ran from police.

3. *What happened to David:* David was ultimately placed in a 9–12 month secure residential juvenile treatment program. He successfully completed the program and returned to live with his mother in the community. At last report, he was scheduled to graduate from high school, but is still in search of employment. He remains on probation.

Chapter nine: Adjudication hearings

The case of Ethan

1. *The hearing officer's decision:* The referee in Ethan's case heard detailed information from Ethan, as well as from his father. Although Ethan provided significant rationale showing that he clearly felt justified in his behaviors, he did admit to the referee that his behaviors met the criteria for being incorrigible. Therefore, the referee declared Ethan a delinquent, and scheduled a dispositional hearing.
2. *The hearing officer's rationale:* The referee noted that Ethan's behaviors were clearly incorrigible; however, he added that he had great concern with the overall dysfunction in the home. He noted Ethan's impulsive behavior and how, during stressful situations, he often fled the home, placing himself at great risk. The referee continued Ethan in nonsecure juvenile detention until counseling services were in place. After that time, he permitted Ethan to return home on home detention, monitored by a tether.
3. *What happened to Ethan:* Ethan was placed on an order for intensive probation with continued tethering. He was ordered to participate in individual and family counseling, submit to random drug screens, and follow all home and school rules. Within the first two months, Ethan had repeatedly violated his probation rules and was then placed in a residential treatment program. He is currently doing well in his program. His father is also very involved and supportive. It is anticipated that Ethan will be released to his father within the next two months.

The case of Johnetta

1. *The hearing officer's decision:* Because Johnetta denied all responsibility and pled not guilty, the hearing officer set the matter for trial at a later date. Several witnesses testified at the trial and the hearing officer ultimately found Johnetta responsible on all delinquent counts. Johnetta was continued in secure detention and the matter was scheduled for disposition three weeks later.
2. *The hearing officer's rationale:* Because Johnetta pled not guilty, the hearing officer had no discretion and had to set the matter for trial.

3. *What happened to Johnetta:* Johnetta was found guilty and placed in a secure 9–12 month residential juvenile treatment program. Her grandmother immediately filed for guardianship, which was awarded shortly after Johnetta was placed. Her grandmother was then able to participate in all family therapy sessions held within the program. With her grandmother's consistent support and encouragement, along with the support of the program's counselors and therapists, Johnetta excelled and was released to her grandmother after nine months. She is currently being monitored by the court on a probationary order.

The case of Jacob

1. *The hearing officer's decision:* Jacob pled guilty at the hearing. The hearing officer accepted his plea and continued him in secure detention, pending the disposition hearing, which was scheduled to take place three weeks later.
2. *The hearing officer's rationale:* The hearing officer made his decision to place Jacob in juvenile detention primarily for safety reasons. He noted great concern for the wellbeing of everyone in the home. Jacob displayed little remorse and has shown disregard for all prior attempts at interventions. The hearing officer felt that Jacob's behavior, while in the community, was too impulsive and dangerous to allow him to return home.
3. *What happened to Jacob:* Jacob was placed in a four-month, highly structured residential boot-camp. In addition to common boot camp expectations and criteria, great focus was placed on individual and family therapy. Jacob's family relationships improved and he also learned to respect authority figures. Jacob has been living at home and attending school within the community successfully for the past six months. The juvenile court recently terminated jurisdiction.

The case of Shayna

1. *The hearing officer's decision:* The hearing officer in Shayna's case accepted her guilty plea and scheduled the matter for disposition three weeks later. He released Shayna to her mother pending the disposition hearing.
2. *The hearing officer's rationale:* The hearing officer's decision to release Shayna pending disposition was because he felt that she had learned a great deal from the short time she spent in juvenile detention. Although her charges were very serious, it was her first offense, she was extremely remorseful, and obviously scared. Her mother

was appropriately involved and supportive. Her mother assured the hearing officer that she would closely monitor Shayna pending disposition.
3. *What happened to Shayna:* Shayna was placed on a six-month probationary period. She was ordered to participate in individual counseling, complete 60 h of youth–community service, pay $20 in restitution (for the movie ticket and snacks), tour the local women's jail, and follow all home and school rules. Shayna quickly complied with all probationary requirements and excelled during the months following her court hearing. She was released from probation at the six-month review hearing.

The case of Austin

1. *The hearing officer's decision:* Austin pled guilty at the hearing. The hearing officer accepted his plea and continued him in secure detention. The disposition was delayed for several weeks purposely to allow for the hearing in the adult court to take place. If the adult court took official jurisdiction over Austin, the juvenile court would then have additional dispositional options.
2. *The hearing officer's rationale:* The hearing officer's primary concern was Austin's safety and wellbeing. Continuing him in secure detention would ensure that he would remain healthy, drug-free and in school. A final decision regarding the juvenile disposition would weigh heavily on the sanctions Austin would receive within the adult court. Ideally, Austin would transition from juvenile detention to either an adult inpatient substance abuse treatment center or jail.
3. *What happened to Austin:* Austin pled guilty to the pending charges for possession of a controlled substance, within the adult system, and was placed in the county jail, with a conditional release to attend intensive substance abuse treatment, among other requirements. The juvenile offenses were then placed on his official juvenile record and the matter was closed.

Chapter ten: Disposition hearings

The case of Jamal

1. *The hearing officer's decision:* The hearing officer ordered Jamal to participate in a 6–9 month residential treatment program, during which time intensive family counseling was ordered. Jamal would also receive individual therapy, participate in school daily (and also in a credit recovery program at school), and learn independent lifeskills. His father was ordered to participate in

all scheduled family therapy sessions and to support Jamal throughout his program. By the time of disposition, Jamal's mother had moved back to the same area, so she too was ordered to participate in family therapy. Sessions were to be held separately with each parent and, on occasion, joint sessions were to be scheduled as well. Jamal's permanent plan would be determined near the completion of his program and be based on the success or lack thereof, in therapy.

2. *The hearing officer's rationale*: The hearing officer placed the highest priority on Jamal's overall well-being and safety. She was also mindful of the possibility that Jamal could simply be manipulating the system or attempting to avoid having to follow his father's rules. She felt certain, however, that if Jamal were returned to his father, he would continue to play truant, which would put him at great risk and affect his progress in school. Placing Jamal in a residential treatment facility would provide a stable, long-term, separate housing arrangement for Jamal to process his feelings, while attending school and maturing. Additionally, all involved parties would have extended time to explore their feelings and concerns without the daily stressors related to residing together. Consistent family therapy over the course of several months would hopefully allow parties to repair and rebuild their relationships.

3. *What happened to Jamal*: Jamal successfully completed the residential program within seven months. His commitment and growth in his program and in therapy was outstanding, but his father's involvement was poor. He failed to attend therapy sessions, failed to return Jamal's phone calls, and failed to consistently take Jamal on earned passes. He did appear on occasion and did take Jamal on a pass or two; however his interaction with Jamal during those passes was minimal. Jamal was able to process his feelings about his father and learn coping methods and conflict resolution skills. Fortunately, Jamal's mother was highly involved. She participated in every possible session, took Jamal on pass and supported him through his transition back into the community. Jamal was released to his mother. He is attending his former high school and is a member of the school's Reserve Officers' Training Corp (ROTC). He is scheduled to graduate in June. He continues to visit with his father on occasion, but their relationship remains strained.

The case of Melissa

1. *The hearing officer's decision*: The hearing officer followed the recommendations given by the

psychologist in the psychological assessment report. The judge placed her on an intensive probation order, and further ordered her to participate in anger management classes and, of course, to attend school regularly. Her parents were referred to parent training classes, and it was strongly suggested to her mother that she establish contact with a local domestic violence program for women.

2. *The hearing officer's rationale*: The judge had concerns about both Melissa and her mother. She wanted to make sure that Melissa would get more frequent contacts with her probation officer, but that she would also receive the assistance of anger management training. The judge also believed that the family issues be addressed and, thus, ordered the parents to go to a parenting program. Furthermore, concerned about domestic violence in the home, she asked the mother to go to the domestic violence shelter in her city.

3. *What happened to Melissa*: Melissa seemed to thrive on intensive probation. She saw her probation officer three times a week, and when the probation officer showed up at school to see Melissa, she always found her in attendance. She began going to an anger management class about a month after her probation started, and she told her probation officer that she enjoyed the classes and was learning a great deal about controlling her feelings and that she is learning to talk about things bothering her. Her parents, somewhat reluctantly, attended a parenting program, and although they didn't think they needed help at first found that the weekly sessions helped them to work together to set rules and establish limits for Melissa and her brother. They told the probation officer that for the first time they agreed on how to handle Melissa if she skipped school. The mother did start going to some counseling sessions at the domestic violence center, and reported that she would use the services of this center if there were more incidents of violence from Melissa's father. At her sixth-month review hearing, the whole family gave positive reports of progress, but the judge decided to keep Melissa on intensive probation for "at least three more months" to ensure that she continued to attend school and to make positive changes.

Chapter eleven: Waiver hearings

The case of Joseph

1. *The hearing officer's decision:* The hearing officer in this matter waived Joseph to an adult court.

2. *The hearing officer's rationale:* The hearing officer placed great weight on the fact that Joseph had

been receiving quality intervention consistently since the age of 4. Additionally, by the time of his last offense, he had exhausted nearly all juvenile court services, which were exceptional and tailored specifically to his specific needs. His mother and other community members provided tremendous support and, despite their efforts, Joseph returned to dangerous, life-threatening behaviors within months of his release. He was a great risk to the safety of others. Community protection was necessary.

3. *What happened to Joseph*: Joseph was sentenced to 6 to 40 years within the adult prison system. He is currently in a medium-level secured facility that houses many young adult offenders.

The case of Jason

1. *The hearing officer's decision:* The hearing officer in this case waived Jason to the adult court.
2. *The hearing officer's rationale:* Although Jason's childhood and upbringing was extremely sad and compelling, it did not excuse or minimize his responsibility or the seriousness of his offenses. He entered several homes through bedroom windows, stole from the home owners and, on one occasion, while in possession of a weapon, molested a young boy. Additionally, Jason never took responsibility for his actions and also never apologized. He appeared to have no remorse. The hearing officer believed that he was at high risk for reoffending. The decision was made with great focus on community protection.
3. *What happened to Jason:* Jason was sentenced to four to twenty years in the adult prison system. He is placed in a maximum-security-level prison.

The case of Kimberly

1. *The hearing officer's decision:* The hearing officer did not waive Kimberly to the adult court. Her case was retained within the juvenile system.
2. *The hearing officer's rationale:* Several factors were considered by the hearing officer in making the decision to not waive Kimberly's case to the adult system. It was her first offense. She ultimately took responsibility for her actions and showed great remorse. She was behind academically. She was a new, young mother. Keeping her within the juvenile system ensured that she would remain geographically close to her family—her source of support—and especially to her daughter. Being housed nearby would allow for frequent visits to hopefully keep their parent–child bond strong. The juvenile system would meet her academic

needs and keep the community safe. Aside from attending high school classes, Kimberly would be able to participate in credit recovery labs to regain school credits she had previously lost. Intensive therapy and counseling would be a priority during her programing and parent education classes would be incorporated as well.

3. *What happened to Kimberly:* Kimberly successfully completed a 9 month, county-based residential treatment program that was located less than 20 miles from her home. While there, in addition to the typical program and therapeutic requirements, she earned nine high-school credits, participated in weekly parent education classes, had regular visits with her daughter, and practiced her parenting skills during her weekend passes. Upon completion of her program, she was released to her mother, who helps care for her young daughter. She enrolled in an alternative community high school and secured part-time employment. She continues to work toward completing her high-school requirements and has remained crime-free.

Chapter twelve: Sentences after a waiver hearing

The case of Dennis

1. *The hearing officer's decision:* The judge sentenced Dennis as an adult to serve 18 months to five years in prison.
2. *The hearing officer's rationale:* The judge had great concern regarding Dennis' history of disrespecting all authority; his mother, school officials, police officers, court personnel, etc. Dennis appeared to have no regard for others, showed no remorse and no desire to change. He was not invested in bettering himself; was not attending school or pursuing employment. The sentence imposed was meant as a harsh consequence for Dennis, but also to ensure safety in the community.
3. *What happened to Dennis:* Dennis continues to serve his prison term. He will not be eligible for parole for another eight months.

The case of James

1. *The hearing officer's decision:* The judge sentenced James as an adult and ordered him to serve five to 15 years in prison.
2. *The hearing officer's rationale:* Although James and his friend did not follow through with their entire plan, they still committed an extremely serious offense; they held loaded guns to the heads of random strangers, ordered them out of their car, and

stole their wallets. Deciding not to steal the car did not lessen the seriousness of the armed robbery that they did commit. The hearing officer appreciated that James was cooperative with the police and also that he expressed remorse. The sentence was on the low end of the sentencing guidelines. It was imposed as a consequence, as well as to protect the community.

3. *What happened to James:* James continues to serve his prison term. He will be eligible for parole in four years.

Chapter thirteen: Violation of probation hearings

The case of Steven

1. *The hearing officer's decision:* The hearing officer accepted Steven's guilty plea to violating his aftercare probation and detained him immediately for his ongoing noncompliance. At the violation of probation disposition, Steven was ordered to complete an additional, more restrictive, boot camp residential treatment program along with substance abuse treatment.

2. *The hearing officer's rationale:* The hearing officer was extremely disappointed with Steven's repeated noncompliance, despite the significant intervention that had already occurred. She believed that the strict discipline of the boot camp program would help Steven learn to respect authority, follow rules and mature.

3. *What happened to Steven:* Steven successfully completed the boot-camp residential treatment program, which included an intensive substance abuse education program. He developed respect, improved his behavior, and also raised his grades. He missed the remainder of his traditional high school years, including his varsity football season, which had great impact on his scholarship eligibility. However, since his release, he has remained crime- and substance-free, and is nearing completion of his high school requirements at an alternative high school.

The case of Christine

1. *The hearing officer's decision:* The hearing officer accepted Christine's guilty plea to violating her probation. He ultimately placed her on an order to complete a 6–9 month residential treatment program and order that she also participate in intensive substance abuse education and treatment.

2. *The hearing officer's rationale:* The hearing officer gave great weight to the severity of Christine's violations (two school suspensions and a positive drug screen) as well as to the short period of time in which they occurred (within the first few weeks). Her school status was not a concern, given that she was often out of school on suspensions and earning several failing grades. Therefore, placing her residentially and requiring her to attend a school within a program would only help her and not jeopardize her progress toward earning high-school credits.

3. *What happened to Christine:* Christine successfully completed the residential treatment program in nine months and was released on probation. She and her family were truly invested in therapy and made great progress. Christine stopped using controlled substances, found new self-worth, and reprioritized her goals. She returned to her home, school and to the cheer team. Her coach has been a great source of support. Christine continues to submit to random drug screens and also attends counseling with her family from home. She will likely be released from probation at the end of the school year.

The case of Donna

1. *The hearing officer's decision:* The hearing officer accepted Donna's guilty plea to violating her probation. He later ordered her to complete a 6–9 month residential treatment program with a focus on individual therapy, anger management, and psychiatric services.

2. *The hearing officer's rationale:* The hearing officer expressed concern regarding Donna's ongoing disrespect and defiance, in addition to her repeated absences. He determined that she was not committed to the day treatment plan. Despite the high level of intervention they provided, it appeared that Donna required a more restrictive environment.

3. *What happened to Donna:* Donna is currently participating in a residential treatment program. She receives great support from her counselors, psychiatrist and her family. Her attitude has improved, and she appears motivated to continue on a more positive path. She is doing well in school, socializing well with the other residents, and working hard to meet her therapy goals. She will likely begin earning day passes to go home soon, and hopefully successfully complete the program within the next six months.

Chapter fourteen: Neglect and abuse hearings

The case of Marissa and her family

1. *The hearing officer's decision:* The hearing officer authorized the petition, took temporary wardship of the children, and placed them immediately in foster care. Their parents were placed on a Parent–Agency Agreement with the Department of Human Services, which outlined specific goals, as well as an expected timeline for completion. Successful compliance with the parent–agency agreement would determine whether their children would be returned, and if so, in what period of time.

2. *The hearing officer's rationale:* The hearing officer had great concern over the father's aggressive nature with the children, both parents' repeated drug use, and mother's drug use throughout pregnancy. He believed there were addiction concerns that needed to be addressed immediately. There was also great concern regarding the situations in the home, involving the use and possession of controlled substances that the children were continuously being exposed to.

3. *What happened to Marissa, Mitchell, Melanie, Emmanuel, and Amy:* The children remain in the custody of their foster parents while their biological parents continue to work on compliance with their parent–agency agreement. Neither parent has been fully compliant. They have each failed to attend various therapy sessions, parenting education sessions, as well as anger management sessions; neither parent has completed substance abuse education, and both have failed to attend the required NA (Narcotics Anonymous) or AA (Alcoholics Anonymous) meetings. The mother has failed four of five drug screens; the father has failed two of three, and has failed to submit to another two. Until they can provide clean drug screens, they will be denied visits with their children. The children are all doing well in foster care and are hopeful to visit their parents soon. At this time, the plan continues to be reunification. However, if the parents' noncompliance continues, the court may change the permanency plan to termination, and schedule the matter for an evidentiary termination hearing.

The case of Andrew and his family

1. *The hearing officer's decision:* The hearing officer authorized the petition, took temporary wardship of the children, and placed them immediately in foster care. Their mother was placed on a parent–agency agreement with the Department of Human Services, which outlined specific goals, as well as an expected timeline for completion. Successful compliance with the parent–agency agreement would determine whether her children would be returned, and if so, in what period of time.

2. *The hearing officer's rationale:* The hearing officer had great concern regarding the safety and well-being of the children. The mother had exhausted resources known to her and was unable to provide them with basic care and/or shelter. The hearing officer had additional concerns regarding the mother's health and ability to obtain medical care related to her pregnancy. The children's health was also at risk.

3. *What happened to Andrew, Aaron, Stephanie, and Elizabeth:* The children remain in the custody of their foster parents while their mother continues to work on compliance with her parent–agency agreement. To date, she has been participating fully. She now resides in a women's shelter and attends a job placement workshop daily. She also participates in therapy, parenting education, substance abuse education, and submits to random drug and alcohol screens. She is allowed supervised visits with her children once per week. They are doing well in foster care. The mother's goals are to continue attending the job placement workshop and make efforts to become employed. She is to secure low-income housing, coordinate government financial assistance, and obtain health insurance for herself and the children. She is to develop a budget to account for living expenses for herself and her children. The matter will be reviewed again in six months. The plan at this time continues to be reunification. Based on the mother's status and progress, the court will determine when her children may be returned.

Chapter fifteen: Review hearings

The case of Thomas

1. *The hearing officer's decision:* At the review hearing, the hearing officer granted the caseworker's request to close Thomas' case successfully and release him from probation.

2. *The hearing officer's rationale:* The hearing officer noted that Thomas had complied with his probation rules and that over the course of the past several months, had developed improved school habits and gained an understanding for the importance of education.

3. *What happened to Thomas:* At the hearing, Thomas told the hearing officer that he was earning better grades and his relationships with his teachers had improved. He was proud of himself and appeared much happier than when he was first referred. During the months that followed, Thomas remained in his father's home, visited with his mother on the weekends, and completed the school year successfully.

The case of Katrina

1. *The hearing officer's decision:* At the review hearing, the hearing officer granted the caseworker's request to close Katrina's case successfully and release her from probation.
2. *The hearing officer's rationale:* The hearing officer noted that Katrina had been involved with the court for over a year. She had successfully completed a very intensive, long-term program, and had put forth great effort the entire time. He also noted that since her release, she has found several sources of support, and learned how to be a support for others as well. She had matured and appeared motivated to continue on her successful path.
3. *What happened to Katrina:* Katrina continues to do well. She is currently completing her senior year and working a part-time job at a restaurant. She is on track to graduate in the spring and plans to attend the local community college so she can remain at home to help her family. She completed driver's education and has her own small vehicle. She continues to gain independence and demonstrate responsibility.

The case of Sarah

1. *The hearing officer's decision:* At the review hearing, the hearing officer granted the caseworker's request to close Sarah's case successfully and release her probation.
2. *The hearing officer's rationale:* The hearing officer was pleased that Sarah had shown genuine investment in her health and education. She was unable to attend a traditional high school and began going to an alternative high school—a new school that could better accommodate her needs. She attended regularly and made great effort to make as much progress as possible prior to her due date. He was also pleased that she participated in parent education and developed relationships with the visiting nurses. Although Sarah's circumstances were not typical, she continued to follow through with educating herself and preparing herself for her next

steps. The hearing officer also commended Sarah's mother for her involvement and support.
3. *What happened to Sarah:* Sarah had a healthy baby boy and is doing well in her role as a young mother. She has not yet returned to school and does not want to continue pursuing employment at this time. Fortunately, her mother is providing for her and her baby's needs, and is willing to continue doing so. Sarah has goals of completing high school and does want to begin working soon. She continues to receive home visits from the public health nurse, and has coordinated other government aid to help her care for her son. She has remained substance-free and has had no additional contacts with the police.

Chapter sixteen: Drug courts

The case of Dian

1. *The hearing officer's decision:* The juvenile drug court judge accepted Dian in the juvenile drug court program, placing her on probation. He also placed her on an alcohol-sensing tether to detect whether she was staying away from alcohol. She was also ordered to attend an AA (Alcoholics Anonymous) program so she could find an older, female sponsor. She and her father were also referred to a family therapist for counseling. Dian was ordered to stay away from any and all parties at which there might be alcohol, and the judge imposed a curfew on her for the first 90 days of her probation. And she was ordered to attend juvenile drug court for weekly updates about her progress.
2. *The hearing officer's rationale:* The juvenile drug court judge believed that Dian needed as many services as possible to counteract the influence of her father and her peers. He also thought that her father possibly needed as many services as Dian, although he couldn't order him to go to AA or family therapy.
3. *What happened to Dian:* Dian was compliant on probation and seemed motivated to succeed in the drug court. She eventually found a female sponsor and became plugged into the recovery community; however, she remained very susceptible to peer pressure and it became evident she'd been holding onto many family secrets which were impeding her progress. Her father's alcohol use could not be ignored and three months into her probation, the judge, as part of Dian's program, required him to submit to regular alcohol blood tests, and he also did the same for Dian. He also strongly suggested that Dian's father get involved in AA. Dian had a few minor setbacks (getting drunk at a party and sneaking alcohol from

her father's liquor cabinet), and, as a result, was assigned several weekends at a juvenile court program for probation violators. But Dian did complete the program successfully in a little over a year.

The case of Jackson

1. *The hearing officer's decision:* Since Jackson was already on probation to the juvenile court, an agreement was reached between the probation department and the juvenile drug court that Jackson's adult charges and probation would be handled through the juvenile drug court— unless or until he failed juvenile drug court. The drug court judge ordered him to test every day for drugs, especially heroin. This was an ongoing order until it was clear that he was no longer hooked on heroin. In addition, he was ordered to go to Narcotics Anonymous group sessions, and was told he needed to report to his probation officer three times a week. He and his parents were ordered to appear weekly in juvenile drug court for progress updates.

2. *The hearing officer's rationale:* The juvenile drug court judge thought that Jackson had a chance to kick his heroin addiction because he had the support of his parents and because Jackson was bright and had been a successful student at one time. Although the judge recognized that heroin addiction is very tough to fight, he thought that with close supervision and the community support offered by the drug court, Jackson had a chance.

3. *What happened to Jackson:* Jackson eventually transitioned to an alternative high school program through which he was offered some credit recovery. He identified himself to his probation officer as a homosexual, and it was clear that he had a significant sexual abuse history that had begun after he started using drugs. At one point, it was learned during probation sessions, he had been prostituted by an older man in the community to make money to feed his drug habit. This led to the man being arrested and charged with prostitution. This, in turn, resulted in a widely publicized trial. Although Jackson was never identified in the media, many of his classmates were aware that he was the victim in the case. Every time this case made additional news, Jackson was at particularly high risk for relapse. Nonetheless, Jackson made slow progress and, eventually, was ordered into psychological counseling to deal with the many mental health issues that surfaced during probation. He eventually picked up adult charges of heroin possession and use after he overdosed, and he was quickly diagnosed by the EMS (Emergency Medical Services) team that arrived at his home after his parents found him unconscious in the bathroom of their home and called 911. Eventually, it became clear Jackson was failing his classes at the alternative high school and that he was not likely to graduate.

Seven months into his juvenile drug court program, his parents called his probation officer to report that he had stolen a number of tools and electronics from home, and they didn't know where he was. That led to a violation of his probation, and the judge felt he had no choice but to transfer him out of juvenile drug court and into adult court. Jackson was arrested by county sheriffs and placed in jail while new charges were filed. He was discontinued from juvenile drug court.

References

Arthur, P.J. and Waugh, R. 2009. Status offenses and the Juvenile Justice and Delinquency Prevention Act: The exception that swallowed the rule. *Seattle Journal for Juvenile Justice* 7(2), 555–576.

Bartollas, C. and Miller, S.J. 2005. *Juvenile justice in America*, 4th edn. Upper Saddle River, NJ: Pearson Education, Inc.

Champion, D.J. 2001. *The American dictionary of criminal justice: Key terms and major court cases (2nd ed.)*. Los Angeles: Roxbury Publishing co.

Champion, D.J. 2010. *The Juvenile Justice System: Delinquency, Processing, and the Law*. Upper Saddle River, NJ: Prentice Hall.

Del Carmen, R.V. and Trulson, C.R. 2006. *Juvenile Justice: The System, Process, and the Law*. Belmont, CA: Thomson Higher Education.

Feld, B.C. 1989. The right to counsel in juvenile court: An empirical study of when lawyers appear and the difference they make. *Journal of Criminal Law & Criminology* 79(4), 1185–1346.

Fuller, J.R. 2013. *Juvenile Delinquency: Mainstream and Crosscurrents*, 2nd edn. New York: Oxford University Press.

Garner, B.A. 2000. *Black's law dictionary (abridged 7th ed.)*. St. Paul, MN: West Group.

Graham v. Florida. 2010. 130 S.Ct. 2011.

Griffin, P. and Torbet, P. 2002. *Desktop Guide to Good Juvenile Probation Practice*. Pittsburg, PA: National Center for Juvenile Justice.

Hess, K. 2010. *Juvenile Justice*, 5th edn. Belmont, CA: Wadsworth.

Houston, J. and Barton, S.M. 2005. *Juvenile Justice: Theory, Systems, and Organization*. Upper Saddle River, NJ: Pearson Education, Inc.

In re Frank H., 337 N.Y.S. 2d 118 1972.

In re Gault, 387, U.S. 1. 1967.

Jackson, M.S. and Knepper, P. 2003. *Delinquency and Justice*. Boston, MA: Allyn and Bacon.

Kent v. United States, 383 U.S. 541. 1966.

Mack, J.W. 1909. The juvenile court. *Harvard Law Review* 23, 104–122.

Mays, G.L. and Winfree, L.T. 2000. *Juvenile Justice*. Boston, MA: McGraw-Hill Higher Education.

Miller v. Alabama, 567 U.S. 2012.

Office of Juvenile Justice and Delinquency Prevention. 2007. Predictors of receiving counseling in a national sample of youth: The relative influence of symptoms, victimization exposure, parent-child conflict, and delinquency. NCJ 220280. Retrieved from http://www.ojjdp.gov/publications/PubAbstract.asp?pubi=242080&ti=&si=&sei=&kw=&PreviousPage=PubResults&strSortby=date&p=&strPubSearch=

Pound, R. 1959. The place of the family court in the judicial system. *Crime & Delinquency* 5(161), 161–171.

Puzzenchara, C., Adams, B., and Hockenberry, S. 2012. Juvenile court statistics 2009. National Center for Juvenile Justice. Retrieved from http://www.ojjdp.gov/pubs/239114.pdf.

Seiter, R.P. 2005. *Corrections: An Introduction*. Upper Saddle River, NJ: Pearson Education, Inc.

Snyder, H.N. and Sickmund, M. 2006. *Juvenile Offenders and Victims 2006 National Report*. Washington, DC: U.S. Department of Justice, Office of Justice Programs, Office of Juvenile Justice and Delinquency Prevention.

Taylor, R.W. and Fritsch, E.J. 2011. Juvenile justice: Policies, programs, and practices, 3rd edn. New York: McGraw-Hill.

The President's Commission on Law Enforcement and the Administration of Justice 1967. *The Challenge of Crime in a Free Society*. Washington, DC: U.S. Government Printing Office.

Vito, G.F. and Simonsen, C.E. 2004. *Juvenile Justice Today*, 4th edn. Upper Saddle River, NJ: Pearson Education, Inc.

Windell, J. 2010. *The Student's Guide to Writing a Criminal Justice Research Paper*, 2nd edn. Dubuque, IA: Kendall Hunt.

Windell, J. 2013. *The American Criminal Justice System: A Concise Guide to Cops, Courts, Corrections, and Victims*. San Diego, CA: Cognella.

Index